PRAISE FOR THE BOOK

'There has never been a more important time to help teachers explore the complexities of teaching sex and relationship education that truly represents the diverse nature of the families and society which young people inhabit. This book will be an invaluable aid to teachers in confidently having sensitive conversations about gender and sexual diversity.'

Dominic Davies, Founder and CEO of Pink Therapy

'Informative, helpful and packed with practical advice for all Key Stages, this is a timely and important book.'

Professor Dame Alison Peacock, Chief Executive
Chartered College of Teaching

'This is an important book in the too-often overlooked field of gender and sexuality education for young people. If appropriately applied, it should lead to a quiet revolution in the physical and mental health of young people who have so unreasonably been disenfranchised by the lack of quality, accessible information in this vital area.'

Professor Christina Richards, Head of Psychology,
Adult Service Tavistock and Portman NHS
Foundation Trust & Visiting Professor of Gender
and Mental Health Regents University London

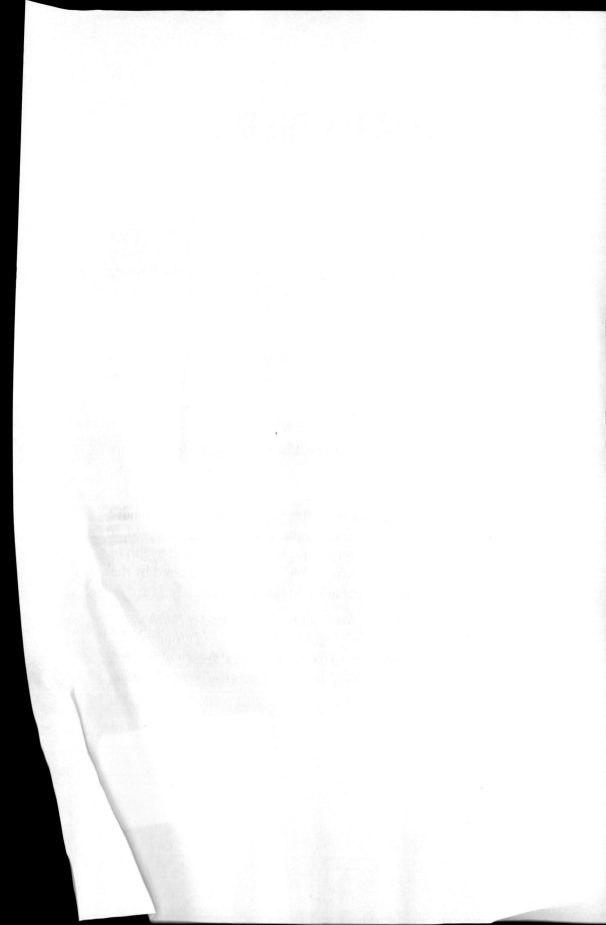

LESSONS
in LOVE &
UNDERSTANDING

JENNI GATES & SCOTT BUCKLER

LESSONS in LOVE & UNDERSTANDING

RELATIONSHIPS, SEXUALITY & GENDER IN THE CLASSROOM

SAGE Publications Ltd
1 Oliver's Yard
55 City Road
London EC1Y 1SP

CORWIN
A SAGE company
2455 Teller Road
Thousand Oaks, California 91320
(0800)233-9936
www.corwin.com

SAGE Publications India Pvt Ltd
B 1/I 1 Mohan Cooperative Industrial Area
Mathura Road
New Delhi 110 044

SAGE Publications Asia-Pacific Pte Ltd
3 Church Street
#10-04 Samsung Hub
Singapore 049483

Editor: James Clark
Assistant editor: Diana Alves
Production editor: Nicola Carrier
Copyeditor: Diana Chambers
Proofreader: Tom Bedford
Indexer: Author
Marketing manager: Dilhara Attygalle
Cover design: Naomi Robinson
Typeset by: C&M Digitals (P) Ltd, Chennai, India
Printed in the UK

Library of Congress Control Number: 2019954165

British Library Cataloguing in Publication data

A catalogue record for this book is available from the
British Library

ISBN 978-1-5297-0894-3
ISBN 978-1-5297-0893-6 (pbk)

At SAGE we take sustainability seriously. Most of our products are printed in the UK using responsibly sourced
papers and boards. When we print overseas we ensure sustainable papers are used as measured by the PREPS
grading system. We undertake an annual audit to monitor our sustainability.

Joan Irene Crumless, 1922–2013

and

James Thomas Crumless, 1954–2008

Remembered for life, learning and love.

CONTENTS

ABOUT THE AUTHORS

 **Jenni Gates** is currently working in private practice as an integrative counselling therapist in Devon, as well as offering online counselling internationally. She is also a counsellor for Pink Therapy and has a special interest in non-binary gender identities. Jenni has a great deal of experience working with young people and families, including delivering relationship and sex education at several schools and education centres across the UK since 2003. She is passionate about mental health and well-being, and believes education is key to a happier, healthier world.

www.jennigatestherapy.co.uk

 **Scott Buckler** has an extensive career in education as a primary and secondary teacher, elearning developer, and as a principal lecturer, having worked for four universities. In recent years, Scott has returned to schools to refresh his practical experience and is currently working towards Chartered Teacher status. Scott has a PhD in anthropology and is widely published in the areas of psychology and education. He is a Chartered Psychologist with expertise in transpersonal psychology and applied educational psychology, two fields that harmonise in the focus on the individual sense of self, a core theme within this book.

www.scottbuckler.com

ACKNOWLEDGEMENTS

No book can be written without the support of many others; indeed, every student, colleague, client and teacher we know has helped shaped this book. We would especially like to express our thanks to James Clark, whose vision and insight in supporting this book has been fundamental, along with Diana Alves, both from Sage Publications (UK). We would also like to thank Nicola Carrier for assisting us with the production stages.

Jenni is eternally grateful for the awesomeness of life-long education, and all the inspirational teachers she has had the privilege (and continues) to experience in the UK and around the world. She gives special thanks to Goedele Liekens, Dominic Davies and Dame Alison Peacock for supporting this book with their incredible expertise and passion for the subject. Last but not least, Jenni would like to thank and pledge love to Bill, Finlay and Annabel who will forever hold a special place in her heart.

Scott would specifically like to thank Jenni for being such a fantastic co-author and for being willing to work on such an ambitious project, while sharing her wealth of experience. He would also like to thank the wonderful students and staff at Holy Trinity Free School, Kidderminster, who every day remind him of how humbling yet rewarding it is to work at such a fantastic school. Finally, thanks to his parents Carol and Richard for their continued love and support, which in a way has shaped this book. And of course, Cameron and Chloe: simply the greatest expression of love and understanding a father could hope to have.

SUPPORT MATERIALS

A website to support this book is available at: www.lessonsinlove.info

FOREWORD

At what age should sexual education start? It is never 'too young' to be learning about relationships and sex as we are born as functioning, thinking beings who express choices, desires, and needs. In these times when sex and new forms of media go hand-in-hand, children will benefit from getting correct and nuanced information about sex. Since sex is omnipresent, sexual education is more important than ever.

Well-informed children have sexual adventures at a later stage and will enjoy these more than children who have been poorly informed. Parents and educators should break through the taboos and throw away their sense of shame about sex. Now is the time to start sexual education in another way. Sex is knocking on every digital door and it is important that children are educated in such a way that they will know when to open that door and when to not.

Lessons in Love & Understanding will be an excellent guide in these matters.

Goedele Liekens, Clinical Psychologist and Sexologist, UNFPA Goodwill Ambassador, TV presenter Sex in Class (Channel 4) and best-selling author.

INTRODUCTION

You are 10 years old. **Puberty** has well and truly started, but you don't know it. Everything feels weird and different, and some of it unpleasant and confusing. You look around at your friends and wonder if they are feeling anything like this. You sense your body changing and look to see if the same changes are visible in others or are noticeable to them in you. You have new thoughts and concerns about how you are viewed socially, and about your thoughts and behaviours being normal. You look at your family at home, wondering if there are any clues there as to what normal really is – this only exacerbates your fears. Why has nobody warned you about any of this? Adults bang on and on about 'growing up' without really explaining what that means. Even teachers at school compare human beings to plant life in attempt to explain **adolescence** and human development. You find this unhelpful as a feeling, thinking, social being with many parts to your individual character and self, and this certainly won't help you form meaningful relationships or improve your ability to understand yourself and the world around you.

You are 50 years old. Your body feels as if it is beginning to slow down as your chemical make-up changes. Everything feels strange and different, and some of it unpleasant and confusing. You look around at your peers and wonder if they are feeling anything like this. You sense your body changing and look to see if the same changes are visible in others or noticeable to them in you. You have new thoughts and concerns about how you are socially and professionally seen, and about your thoughts and behaviours being normal. You think of your family, past and present, wondering if there are any clues there as to what normal really is – this exacerbates your fears. Why has nobody warned you about any of this? You hear about people going through 'the change of life' without really understanding what that means for them or for you. Nobody ever taught you about this, at school or beyond. You have no idea what life after 50 entails, despite having heard and seen lots of analogies relating to 'maturing' nature: flora and fauna. But as an emotionally intelligent social being with many facets to your unique **identity**, you rather hope your life and its meaning is slightly more nuanced than that of a potted bamboo plant.

As this book went to print, existing Relationship and Sex Education (RSE) training for teachers included a little bit on **Lesbian**, **Gay** and **Bisexual** (LGB) relationships for secondary schools, but often nothing on **gender identity**; certainly nothing on **intersex** conditions, **queer** culture or different types of relationships. The 'Relationships Education, Relationships and Sex Education (RSE) and Health Education: Statutory guidance for governing bodies, proprietors, head teachers, principals, senior leadership teams, teachers' 2019 policy (which, to save word space, we will just refer to throughout as RSE 2020, as September 2020 is when the policy needs to have been implemented) suggests that we must be more inclusive and include all of this, although it is frustratingly vague on not giving any guidance on age and stage when different areas of RSE should be delivered. And so this book was born. Nobody would expect a teacher to teach a maths class without having been trained to do so, and certainly would not if the teacher had never had a lesson in maths themselves, let alone a qualification in the subject. So why would we treat this massively important subject any differently? The result of this neglect is that everybody, from the 4-year-old nursery pupil to the 64-year-old experienced teacher, gets stressed and confused about sex and **gender**, with neither having any formal teaching on all-inclusive RSE. Many well-educated, well-meaning professionals and parents make a good attempt at their version of social education. Yet inevitably this is biased by their own cultural norms and belief systems, and so this feels unfitting, and even at times offensive to others with differing belief systems and alternative perspectives. Panic breeds, fear sets in and many of us do the very British and polite thing of doing and saying nothing in case we offend anybody. And, after all, it can be massively uncomfortable talking about relationships and sex. Isn't gender and **sexuality** just a whole new realm of awkwardness?

When you stop and think about it: where did your relationship and sex education come from? How did you come to explore your current self-identity, if you ever did? What are your relational needs? Have you ever celebrated your gender? Have you ever learnt about your sexuality and the true 'normalities' around sexual desire, **fantasy**, behaviours, emotions and the difference between them? The trouble is that prior to becoming RSE subject-matter experts, we as authors had never been provided with any educational insight outside of the specialist field. While we had some rudimentary science lessons and a brief talk around bodily function, the concept of gender was only introduced at university when we considered what it meant to be female and male (**non-binary** and gender queer apparently didn't exist back then). Furthermore, we were never formally taught anything about sexuality at school or university. So, is it any wonder that we are all fumbling around in the dark (and not doing very much) with RSE? Yet, this is so important to every single one of us, universally. As such, in this book we are going to share with you the well-kept secrets to a healthy and respectful Relationship and Sex Education. Our aim is to provide you with well-researched and safe methods of teaching this vital and important part of social education, across all cultures and levels of educational need. In doing this, we invite you on a journey of self-discovery, as once we are in a position to be aware of our own personal stance, blind spots and assumed ideas, we can think more openly about the content of what we deliver in the classroom.

Studying relationships, sex, sexuality and gender identity is about learning who we are and how we interact with others. Throughout our lives we have many different types of relationship and ways in which we connect and communicate with other beings. In fact, we could have written this book purely about human relationships, but this would take the focus away from the unique nature of humans as individuals, as 'relationship' encourages us to think in labels and socially constructed groupings. Again, we are wishing to move away from this and to deconstruct the collective identity labels, in order to reveal the naked truth about relationships and sex, and demystify sexuality and gender identity.

As teachers and educators, the principle of aiding pupils to understand themselves and the world around them, in an appropriate way, is our core mission. You already have all the skills and expertise in doing so, yet are let down by the culture of shame around relationships, sex, gender and sexuality. This has created an unfortunate and unnecessary tension around delivery of the subject of Relationship and Sex Education (RSE) and on statutory guidance on what exactly should be delivered to whom and by whom. We live in a world where not just **LGBTQI**+ matters are taboo and not openly discussed, but also relationships, sexuality and gender as a whole.

In order to produce a clear and coherently structured guide for teaching and facilitating all-inclusive RSE, the obvious starting place is in ensuring that we are all speaking/understanding the same language. Relationship- and sex-speak can be confusing, intimidating and a bit of a turn-off, regardless of age or experience. Be it in the playground or within a professional academic setting, terminology not only changes but has cultural differences, making it completely impossible to fully keep up with, let alone know what is politically correct, or appropriate to use within the classroom. It is important that we define our use of language within this book. Words like 'sex' have various meanings, and this alone could cause misinterpretation, and frequently does. So, we have provided you with some basic definitions and a Glossary of terms for your general understanding and reference. We appreciate that it is not possible for you to look up many RSE terms from your school computer, so we hope this is a useful tool. The Glossary is there for you to refer to at any time you wish, although it may be advisable to have a little look now. Please note that words **emboldened** in the text are described in the Glossary.

Having returned from the Glossary, we invite you to take a moment to stop and notice how you feel. What is going on for you, at this moment? There are no wrong answers, and any range of feelings, thoughts and emotions, and physiological responses are possible. It can feel a bit like looking up the naughty words in a dictionary when you've first learnt to read. Keep this in mind, because we're trusting that the majority of you did not go straight out and have sex because you'd read the dictionary definition, nor did you turn into a giant penis having looked up the word 'penis'. We do not become what we read. We use information to inform our choices, along with the safe teaching that we receive from our families, communities and education professionals, *when* that teaching is made available to us. The danger comes when this type of education is *not* available to us. Where do human beings go then? The internet, **pornography**, social experimentation – all without the guidance of those previously named guardians of developmental well-being. So, let's not be scared by all the terminology. Let's also be mindful that many of these labels raise strong feelings and opinions for people. There are various associations and interpretations for the terminology and jargon listed that we must always be sensitive towards. Some phrases are outdated, inaccurate and potentially offensive. We have tried to be careful in our use of language (and general content) within this book, so please accept our sincere apology if you read something here that you find inappropriate. We have avoided the use of scare quotes to allow this book to be as accessible as possible, and hope we have set the pitch accordingly.

Our hope is, having leapt over language barriers and cringed away our awkwardness, we have already improved our author–reader connection and communication in this book. We will engage in learning far more effectively now that we are familiar with a common language. This is also true of your teacher–pupil learning relationship. Throughout this book, you will notice that we encourage that our author–reader relationship should be reflective or a parallel to your teacher–pupil relationship. The aim is in giving autonomy to the learner. This leads to another important point about labels. The Glossary is only a guide to commonly perceived definitions of the terminology listed (note, words in bold throughout this book appear in the glossary). We have examined that it is crucial not to make any assumptions and that labels do not define the unique individual. In real life this means finding out what the individual means by the labels they choose to describe themselves. Remember, the individual is the expert on *their* self. Teaching this subject relies on a shared learning process and willingness to use all the knowledge within the classroom. This can be a frightening concept for teachers and parents, as we have an inbuilt expectation of holding the wisdom and expertise in leading children, young people and students in their quest for learning all worldly matters. But this is about the pupil understanding their *self*. It is about each individual (including us as readers and authors) understanding one's own self and unique identity and how this 'self' fits alongside others in the wider world. There is a *personal* responsibility here for each and every one of us, as you are the world-leading expert on *you*. You are not the expert on any other individual, and it is not your responsibility to make, mould, shape or fashion the core of any other human being, be it your own birth child or your student. That bit belongs to them and us all as individuals; we have personal expertise on our own selves. This leads to the natural starting point for this book: understanding the self before we go on to explore gender, relationships, sex and sexuality, and set all of this in the context of the RSE 2020 guidance while making it come alive in the learning space, with guidance for policy, good practice and support – as well as suggested Lessons in Love and Understanding.

What this book is *not* trying to do is provide a linear, calculated, diagnostic, prescriptive type of tool. We are not in the business of advising: if pupil identifies/presents with A, then do B. One of the central messages is that as individuals, our core being is not defined by any one way of identifying. As unique beings, the labels that we use to help others understand something of our identity can never describe our own unique self or experience.

It's easy to instruct 'don't judge a book by its cover'; however, teaching and learning how to actually do that is not so easy. As human beings, it is a survival mechanism to constantly make judgements. This is part of our biological make-up and we do this before even leaving the womb. Fear keeps us safe from perceived threat, although fear also disables us from healthy development, when our perception of real threat is false. If we are too fearful of opening the book because we were put off by the cover, we lose the ability to make any true judgement of the book, as we don't know what its content is. RSE is much like this. Many of us have fears around what the content might be, so we leave that book on the shelf, feeling that this is the safest option. The law says we need to change that, and it's going to be an exciting and liberating journey that starts right here. Learning about who we are as individuals, and feeling safe, secure and confident in being who we are, on this planet, is vital. We can only achieve this by understanding a full spectrum of possibility and learning to respect ourselves and others, should we find we are similar or different in our personal identities. There is always fear at the root of hate. We live in a world where there still exists a great fear around open discussion on gender identity and sexuality. Our hope is that this book reduces the reader's fears or vicarious fears in order that you feel safe, secure and confident in leading and facilitating relationship and sex education for all.

1

UNDERSTANDING THE SELF

CONTENTS

- Why this chapter?
- The self
- Self-concept
- The importance of nurturing the self
- Perspective
- What do we really know?
- Conclusion

CHAPTER OBJECTIVES

- To understand the importance of an individual's self.
- To appreciate that there are a range of competing perspectives that attempt to explain the self.
- To explain how self-esteem is affected by the interplay of the self-image and the ideal self.
- To consider approaches to nurturing a student's sense of self.
- To understand how perspectives are unique and how they can be challenged.

WHY THIS CHAPTER?

The purpose of this book, and indeed the current focus on relationships and sex education, is that of the individual: how can a child or young person form and develop meaningful and rewarding relationships through their life and perhaps from this, develop a sexual relationship when appropriate? Consequently, the individual is at the heart of this book and we would like to think similarly, at the heart of education.

Take any individual and consider what makes them unique. What makes you unique? How would you describe yourself to another person? Why are you who you are? Superficially, we may define ourselves by our name and what we do. Some may proceed to analyse this from a range of perspectives such as their relationships (sister/brother, parent, partner, friend) to more detailed analysis such as those listed on a social media profile (a team-playing, keen golfing, Exeter City supporting, real-ale appreciating, Ed Sheeran fanatic). If we take ten personal attributes (such as favourite food, hobby, favourite colour), with ten different choices for each, there would be ten billion possible combinations making you truly unique. What we choose to share might depend on the situation and the meaning it might have in relation to whom we share with. However, within education, we tend to group students and ensure conformity for the smooth running of a school, suppressing the expression of individuality, unless the school has a progressive philosophy. Consequently, labels describing relationships, gender and sexuality are often only shared on a need-to-know basis, being deemed to be more personal than labels of profession or sporting interests. Yet in shedding away these labels of identity, what truly makes you, you? What animates the body you are encased in? Who is that individual expression of wonderfulness reading this book, here and now? Welcome to 'the self'.

THE SELF

What actually is 'the self'? It's funny that we implicitly understand what is meant by 'the self', yet in trying to define it there are many problems. While dictionary definitions may explain what the self is, they lack the depth and scope needed to truly portray what it is. While we define ourselves through labels that relate to our identity, the self is really a first-person perspective on our consciousness – that is, an awareness of our existence. It is what we think and feel. However, this does not move us much closer to defining what the self really is.

Philosophers, psychologists and sociologists have made varying attempts to define the self and explain what it is and how it operates, from different perspectives. As educators, our discipline is multidisciplinary, where we make sense of the individual student and how best to facilitate their learning, requiring an understanding of all such academic fields. While philosophers attempt to identify what the truth of the self is, psychologists attempt to explain how it functions, whereas sociologists attempt to explain how it is shaped in relation to others. Theologists in turn attempt to explain how it connects us to the divine, which links the self with concepts of the soul. While each group has its own approach, even within groups, there are diverse perspectives to illuminate what the self is and how it functions. However, there is still no singularly accepted theory as to what constitutes the self.

Taking just the psychological perspective, there are various fields in psychology such as the psychodynamic, behaviourist, and humanistic, among others, each with numerous theorists. Within your teacher training days, you would almost definitely have come across Abraham Maslow's hierarchy of needs and probably Carl Rogers' heliotropic approach to self-actualisation; you may also have covered Sigmund Freud's id, ego and superego. However, what do these mean in relation to your daily practice? Can we honestly say that we embed such principles to inform our teaching, and that we fully appreciate the dynamic tension of each student's id and ego? Furthermore, what is the practical application of such theories when discussing relationships or sex education? For example, understanding the relationship between fulfilling our needs to sustain our existence (such as the physiological needs of shelter, food and water) before we progress to form relationships is understandable. Yet Maslow places the need for sex at the same level of physiological needs such as food. When was the last time you ate? When was the last time you had sex? Models like this can be useful to consider where our own priorities lie and the importance of relationships and how these fit within the wider sphere of our lives.

There are many other psychological theories of the self, such as Jerome Bruner's transactional self or Mihaly Csikszentmihalyi's transcendent self. Some philosophers such as Derek Parfit argue that there is no such thing as 'the self': instead, what we deem as the self is just a bundle of experiences and sensations, threaded together through memory to provide an illusion of the self.

This latter perspective, of whether the self exists or not, is a central theme within philosophy. Aristotle discussed the relational soul; David Hume and Friedrich Nietzsche suggested that the self is an illusion formed by sensory processes. Others such as René Descartes asked whether we actually exist or whether we are controlled by a malicious demon who induces a hallucination of the world to mislead us from reality, much in the same way as the film *The Matrix*. As teachers, the malicious demon is multifaceted: deadlines, workload, resourcing, tables, progression data, and the like.

The sociological perspective considers how the self is shaped and influenced by others – for example, Charles Cooley proposed the 'looking-glass self', or our perception of how we think we appear to others. This is considered through imagining how we look to other people, then imagining other people's judgements based on how the individual thinks these people view them. From this, we develop our sense of self through responding to this perceived judgement by others. A similar theorist is George Herbert Mead and his theory of symbolic interactionism, whereby through interacting with others, we develop our identity along with being able to empathise with others. A different theorist is Erving Goffman and his dramaturgical analysis, or how we constantly review the roles we play when interacting with others.

In trying to form a friendship or relationship with another person, from a sociological perspective, it is essential to ensure that you present yourself appropriately for the situation while trying to find what you have in common with one another. Within the classroom, encouraging students to think about their interpersonal relationships and helping others to feel at ease through conversation is fundamental to relationship and sex education. This is important, especially in a world where many young people capture and edit everything on camera and interact with false perceptions of self on social media. Consequently, the classroom may be one of the only places where a student has the opportunity to develop social skills. This is similarly important for students who are home-schooled, even if they interact with others in online classrooms. Many home-school networks have a daily opportunity for children to meet with their peers in person to help foster social interaction. However, for young people experiencing mental health concerns, stress in adolescence or perhaps gender discomfort or **dysphoria**, this is often not so simple and they are confined to the relative safety of the online world, which is less stressful than direct social contact which can cause a great deal of distress. So, there are definite benefits to online interactions, especially in bringing social connectivity to those who otherwise might become isolated.

From a theological perspective (and we use the term to encompass religion more broadly), perspectives of the self differ: concepts of the self as an animated soul are found within Hinduism (the *atman*) and in Islam (the *nafs*), although Buddhism asserts that there is no such thing as the self (through their concept of *anattā*). Needless to say, the multitude of perspectives surrounding the self vary within and between religions.

A further model that truly encapsulates the self is that suggested by Professor Peg O'Connor, who related the search for the authentic self as akin to finding a unicorn: neither exist or are ethereal and unknowable in nature (O'Connor, 2014) while Synott (2016) relates the self to a chameleon: ever changing depending on circumstances.

From this brief tour of the self we hope that you appreciate that the self is central to the array of diverse relationships we hold with people: that there is diversity in gender and sexual identities that do not affect an individual's sense of self. By this, is anyone's sense of self any more important than another's? Who's to say what is right or wrong about how a person identifies or expresses their unique sense of self? Think about your self-image (a term we will explore further later on in this chapter). What clothes do you decide to wear to work (such as smart business attire)? What do you wear at home (such as geek-chic to goth)? Are you a member of any clubs or activities that help define who you are and that you have a sense of pride in belonging to? This could be a sports club, a taste in music, and so forth. An empowering activity is to take the time to develop a collage about what is important to you and who you are: an activity equally beneficial for students to engage with.

Of course, how we define ourselves, and what we share with others, is rather more nuanced. For example, if you met a new person in the staff room and they were to introduce themselves, they would be unlikely to say 'Hi, I'm Cecilia. I identify as a British, **pansexual** female (I prefer she/her pronouns), a working single parent, a primary school teacher with a specialism in art, a Roman Catholic, a vegan, a Manchester United supporter, and a super fan of the Kardashians'.[1] Even if all those things were of great importance to Cecilia, and she was keen to share them with you, she would not be telling you anything that reflected or described her core being. The important information you may, however, receive in this interaction is your impression and judgements based on your own internalised ideas about the subgroups with which she identifies or feels she belongs. Your impressions do not define Cecilia. However, if Cecilia feels unaccepted, isolated, rejected or unseen by others who have shown a negative response towards any of those parts of her perceived identity, her core being may feel threatened.

An aspect to acknowledge is that as teachers, we can feel threatened about understanding others' sense of self. This is understandable. It may come from a fear of saying the wrong thing or providing the wrong advice, or it may be that we disagree with how others identify. In returning to the psychological perspective, we may feel threatened due to our upbringing, our beliefs, our values, and so on. Freud's defence mechanisms are one way of thinking about our reactions, some of which are briefly explained below through a work perspective.

---

[1] The voices used in this book are from our wider professional networks and not from any student, client or colleague we work with or have worked with previously.

- Suppression (teacher may hold back on teaching RSE to the level required as the subject brings back painful memories of personal relationships that are safer buried).
- Denial (teacher has the belief that sex before **marriage** is sinful and so would rather not acknowledge that this occurs in reality to avoid having to think about it).
- Avoidance (teacher takes a day off sick to avoid in-house training on RSE as they find it awkward to the point that it does make them feel ill).
- Dissociation (teacher finds a task or concept hard at staff meeting, so starts to daydream in an attempt to lose their connection with the world around them).
- Projection (teacher dislikes their new head of year, but instead of accepting that, projects this to the feeling that the head of year dislikes them and is unkind).
- Introjection (teacher believes that a critical point made about them by another student or teacher is valid, internalising and accepting the comment as valid).
- Rationalisation (teacher attempts to justify their omission of relationship education by suggesting that it is not age appropriate for their class).

Although there are many defence mechanisms, of which we have only included a few, consider how these could relate to the teaching and learning of RSE such as dissociation in a lesson which may make a student feel uncomfortable. By understanding the *concept* of the self we can help children develop their own sense of self. This is fundamental to our approach to teaching children about relationships and sex: if they are insecure in who *they* are, how can they be secure in establishing healthy relationships? Furthermore, through appreciating that selves differ, this should help facilitate students' understanding of what is *real* in terms of identity, and what this means in relationships with others and in wider society.

SELF-CONCEPT

Although defining the self is difficult, it is easier to understand related ideas such as self-esteem or the self-concept. This is similar to knowing how to drive a car but without the full mechanical understanding of what happens under the bonnet, or why we need to protect our skin from the sun without a full understanding of what happens at the molecular level over an extended period of time.

The self-concept is our personal evaluation of our self and comprises three elements: self-image, self-esteem and the ideal self. Our self-image relates to how we describe ourselves (similar to the introduction to this chapter). The self-image encompasses aspects such as our physical description, social roles, personality traits, and existential statements – e.g. 'I'm a spiritual being'. Self-esteem is the evaluation of ourselves or a personal judgement of how worthy we are compared to our perception of our ideal self. A low self-esteem is characterised by a lack of confidence, worrying about what others may think, pessimism, and so forth, while a high self-esteem is characterised by the opposite, such as being confident in one's own abilities, not worrying about other's perceptions, optimism and self-acceptance. Finally, self-image is descriptive, self-esteem is evaluative. If our self-image differs considerably to our ideal self, this impacts on our self-esteem. Consequently, we need either to boost our self-image or lower our perception of our ideal self in order to feel a greater sense of self-esteem.

Within the classroom, as teachers we can help develop a child's self-image through encouraging them to consider who they are and, from this, their uniqueness. We can also help to challenge any negative perceptions, providing examples where possible to support their self-image. If, for example, a child says that they are no good at maths, we could encourage analysis of this statement and identify what it is they need to work on (such as balancing equations), while importantly stressing the areas they excel with (such as simplifying equations). Additionally, we can support children through identifying and reviewing their ideal self. Have they clarified what they want to achieve and, from this, the steps to achieve it? Such a solution-focused approach may take different guises, from learning or skills ladders, to target sheets, and so on.

If we extend this into the area of gender identity, a child may not associate with what society means by male or female. They may identify as a different gender from their 'sex' as listed on their birth certificate. Consequently, their ideal self will be far removed from their self-image which would understandably impact considerably on their self-esteem. From this, they may withdraw from social contact with either gender as they do not feel they belong. This is explained by Stephan.

I haven't a clue who I am. I don't fit in with either group. About a year back, maybe a bit more than that, me and my mates went swimming. I only went 'cos there was a girl I like going. It was only a small group of us going from our form and I've always liked her. But when we were there I just, kinda, avoided them . . . not just her and her mates, but also my mates. I didn't feel part of either group. It was weird. I just watched them from the pool side. The girls were having a right laugh and Katie, who I fancied, looked well fit. But I realised it wasn't that I wanted her . . . I wanted to *be* like her, I mean, really. I wanted her body. I was like frozen. I didn't want to be with the boys and would have felt weird just mixing with the girls. I didn't belong to either the boys or girls and this really hit me. I still don't feel I belong and hate myself for this. I hate my body, and wish I'd been born female, or without a cock, or just not like this. (Stephan, age 15)

From Stephan's account, the tension they feel is profound, not just the dissatisfaction and hatred of their body, but because they are unable to associate with either males or females. Furthermore, Stephan's conflict highlights other aspects that affect their self-concept. According to Michael Argyle (1973/2008), there are four main influences on the self-concept: the reaction of others (what people say or do to us), comparison to others (how we think we are in relation to others, such as academic performance), social roles – for example, certain social roles carry greater prestige such as a being surgeon or Olympic athlete, as opposed to being a teacher – and identification (or how we identify with positions we occupy or the groups we belong to; see Figure 1.1) .

In the classroom, each of these areas can be supported. If, for example, a child takes a comment critically, we can encourage them to consider whether the comment has any foundation or whether it was used to elicit a prescribed response. In relation to comparison to others, we can encourage a child to consider how they have developed over a period of time by reviewing their work at the start of term opposed to comparing to others. We can also encourage children to challenge the people idolised in the media, providing others as role models who do not have PR agents and a huge number of 'likes'. In relation to social roles, stereotypes can be challenged. For example, being unemployed may be socially stigmatising, yet many famous people have

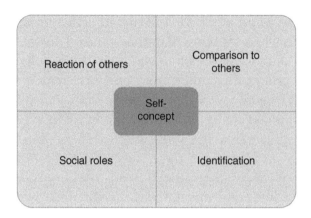

Figure 1.1 Four main influences of self-concept (adapted from Argyle, 1973/2008)

spent time without employment: George Orwell, J.K. Rowling, Walt Disney, Harrison Ford, Steve Jobs. In returning to Stephan, if he did confide in you, the strategies listed here would not be sufficient to help resolve his deteriorated self-concept. However, we will guide you further on in the book on how to support students who do disclose.

Children's sense of self can be fragile for a range of reasons. In order to safely explore who they are and how they relate to the world, and in order that their self-image and ideal-self are relatively balanced, it is important that we challenge the perceptions of others, limiting the comparison with others and challenging stereotypes from social roles to enable the child to be happy in who they are. For example, are all scientists predominantly male, robed in white lab coats, wearing glasses, with wild hair? If you have never asked students in the primary phase to draw a scientist, please do.

THE IMPORTANCE OF NURTURING THE SELF

As professionals, we are aware that each child is unique: that each is a fragile being in our care for a period of time during the school day. What concerns us is how to help them on their way as a person and as a learner, in that order. After all, if a child feels insecure, they are not going to learn effectively.

A child can be harmed in so many ways during their lifetime and, as teachers, we need to limit any further damage, perhaps attempting to resolve any wounds to their sense of self that have previously been inflicted. While we may be unable to fully explain what the self is, inherently we understand what it means to feel valued, encouraged, secure and nurtured. Consequently, we would suggest that although the Government may want us to focus on teaching subjects, our primary role should be to nurture each individual in our class, to encourage a healthy sense of self, and from this, to focus on the learning. As teachers, though, we need to weave such nurturing in with facilitating learning, given the demands of a jam-packed timetable.

Many of the strategies that teachers use in the classroom are central to nurturing the child's sense of self. Although there are explicit frameworks commonly found in schools across the country (such as Carol Dweck's 'Growth Mindset'), how often are they used or referred to? Are children expected to look at the poster and then implement the strategies with little guidance or reinforcement? A core problem with such acronyms and models is that they look good on a professional development course, yet they can often be far removed from the real, everyday world of the classroom.

Our aim is not to provide another model to consider or implement. The focus of this book is on teachers developing a sense of autonomy by taking ownership of their approach to teaching relationships and sex education through flexible strategies. Table 1.1 is a list of some of these developed from our years of professional practice. It is not exhaustive and we would actively encourage you to discuss these with colleagues and to consider additional strategies. Go through this list (they are in no particular order), tick the ones that you already do and highlight two others you will attempt in your classroom.

Table 1.1 Strategies for nurturing the self within the classroom

	I do this	I will do this
Teach children to breathe abdominally as a way of calming and focusing the mind.		
Do not label a child; highlight their strengths.		
Develop a 'can do' mentality through providing an appropriate skill/challenge balance.		
Speak to each child daily (not just when you call the register). Enquire about their hobbies, interests, pet – anything. Engage in a dialogue and really listen.		
Focus on process goals (how the child feels they are doing) as opposed to outcome goals (e.g. a score on a test) or performance goals (e.g. comparison of a score this week to a score last week).		

(Continued)

Table 1.1 (Continued)

	I do this	I will do this
Speak kindly and value the individual.		
Create a safe, secure, calm classroom.		
Encourage problem solving.		
Encourage exploration: do they always need a 'right answer'.		
Encourage self-evaluation.		
Encourage the child to express their feelings through talking, drawing, colouring, doodling, and so forth.		
Promote mutual respect.		
Are you setting a good example of a fully functioning human? If not, who can you talk to for support?		
Are you smiling, genuinely?		
Are you having fun? Are they?		
Praise effort, not results.		
Teach cognitive restructuring (or positive affirmations, auto-suggestion).		
Celebrate difference: interests, celebrations, TV shows, favourite music, and so forth.		
Facilitate thinking.		
Encourage imagination.		
Enjoy being with children.		
Name the child's strengths – they may not be aware of them.		
Laugh with the class.		
Be authoritative, not strict.		
Be prepared to show and share your mistakes.		
Listen to the child: what are they really saying?		
Facilitate intrinsic motivation for personal satisfaction as opposed to rewards or sanctions.		

We hope that through reading this list, you are aware of how fantastically supportive you are in developing children's sense of self; there are probably few, if any, that you do not do. However, seeing a list such as this may help you appreciate what you do implicitly every day.

Earlier in this chapter we introduced the concept of the self and provided a brief overview of how different academic disciplines have attempted to explain the self. We have then taken a far more pragmatic approach in discussing how the developing child's sense of self can be supported.

Within this book, especially in Chapters 2, 3 and 4, we will be introducing a range of perspectives that some may feel are contentious.

By this we mean that there may be readers of this book, other teachers or governors, students who we work with, or indeed their parents, who will challenge what is presented. What is important to remember is that this is *their* perspective. Our purpose in writing this book is to provide an informed approach to teaching the multitude of aspects of RSE and encourage an open discussion about supporting individuals, not necessarily who they represent, but their individual sense of self – after all, is your sense of self any more important than another person's?

Central to our respective backgrounds is the ability to challenge perspectives. Whether counselling clients, facilitating therapeutic support groups, holding doctoral seminars, or teaching at A-level through to teaching a Year 2 class, perspective is an inescapable and profound feature of our professions.

PERSPECTIVE

We would like to invite you to consider what Figure 1.2 represents.

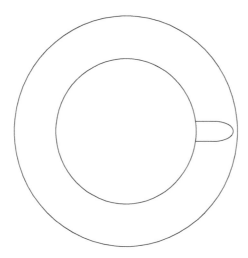

Figure 1.2   Perspective: what does this drawing represent?

Having used this example with students aged 6 to 60, answers tend to relate to an overhead view of a cup and saucer, a washing-machine door, a snow person, a hat with a ribbon, a dial on a cooker. Or is it just two concentric circles and a parabolic arch? Out of these, whose answer is correct or the most correct?

A common theme throughout education should be to challenge perspectives. This is implicit when analysing different characters within a story, considering the motivations between the Cavaliers and the Roundheads in the English Civil War, or evaluating competing theories that explain the causes of psychopathology on an A-level psychology course. However, is the challenging of perspectives only relevant in certain subjects and not transferable to the outside world? How often do we see dualistic, two-sided arguments in the media? Indeed, are the media guilty of causing such dualisms (just reflect for a moment on the Brexit debacle which we hope will have been resolved by the time this book is published). It appears that the more unstable the world becomes, the more we cling tightly to our perspective of what is 'right', followed by 'If I'm right, you're wrong' modes of thinking. As with education, the provision of alternate perspectives is important with appropriate discussion. This is as true when discussing the origins of the universe, or the best way of making scones, to the various relationships that are evident in our society.

Within educational establishments nationally, a common mission statement should be, 'We will not tell you what to think; we will guide you how to think.' Opposed to the focus on correct answers or model ways of obtaining 20 marks on an essay question, the ability to challenge perspectives should be rewarded. From challenging perspectives, new ways of thinking or working can be established, which in turn could lead to new inventions or adaptations of existing ones. Of course, there is a fine line between the freedom of speech while being respectful of others' perspectives, and that of becoming offensive, where one belief system is seen as 'better' than another.

The flexibility to challenge perspectives demonstrates an advanced level of thinking opposed to the dualistic right/wrong debates. The educational psychologist William Perry (1970) proposed a nine-stage model of thinking that individuals progress through to understand knowledge. At the lowest level is the dogmatic stage of 'I'm right, you're wrong', through to the highest level where an individual can be committed to a perspective, yet respect other perspectives, while being open to evaluate new evidence and from this, reconsider their perspective, or find a way to harmonise perspectives, a so-called 'middle ground'. Consequently, we are not asking you to believe uncritically every word we write in this book (nor any other, for that matter).

Instead, we ask you to consider what resonates with your perspective and if something doesn't resonate, to engage in a dialogue to seek a greater understanding.

WHAT DO WE REALLY KNOW?

We tend to grasp what we perceive as truths for a variety of reasons. If something comes along that challenges our perspectives, it is easier to resort to our default position than to accept a change of perspective. From a psychological perspective, Piaget's accommodation and assimilation resonate. With assimilation, a new idea fits in with existing ideas, while with accommodation, a new idea changes an existing idea.

For example, if you were sitting late at night in your room working at the computer on your end-of-year reports and out of the corner of your eye you see a dark figure. You turn to look but only see your normal room. This could be explained through assimilation that you think you have seen something 'weird' as you believe in ghosts. Alternately, you may seek an explanation and search for the 'corner of the eye phenomena', realising that your apparition is explained through visual substitutions, the peripheral drift illusion. Consequently, you have accommodated the information to change your perspectives on a suspected ghostly sighting.

A thought experiment is a hypothetical situation to encourage divergent thinking. Thought experiments (see Lessons in Love & Understanding 1 at the end of this chapter) can be used to help challenge perspectives, encouraging new insights by rearranging information to promote thinking. They can challenge or confirm theories or establish new theories, and are commonly used in philosophy, psychology, computing, law and history, among other subject areas. In the context of this book, thought experiments can help in understanding others' perspectives on relationships, gender or sex. One well-known thought experiment was proposed by Ludwig Wittgenstein. Imagine that everyone is given a box that only they can look inside. Inside everyone's box is a 'beetle'. Everyone refers to their item within the box as a beetle, but nobody can share what is inside their box with anyone else. Consequently, we only know that it is a beetle by referring to our own box. It is possible that everyone has the same 'beetle' in their box; alternately, everyone could have a completely different item or no item at all.

The purpose of this thought experiment is that we refer to concepts that others have no access to. In other words, is my experience of sensing the taste of a strawberry the same as yours? As such, we cannot know another person's mind, what they're experiencing, or their unique perspective. In relation to relationships and sex education, our 'beetle' is unique to us very much like our 'self'. Is it appropriate to dismiss anyone else's beetle as being inferior to yours? Is your beetle ultimately more rewarding than another person's? Have you the right to dismiss anyone's beetle as it is not the right sort of beetle?

CONCLUSION

The purpose of this chapter is to establish a strong foundation from which to explore the themes within this book. As teachers, working with a class of individuals is rewarding yet nuanced. Each student is unique and will have a different understanding of their gender and sexual identity, what their relationships mean, and so on. They will have different perceptions of what is appropriate and what is inappropriate. Some of this may be based on how they have been influenced by culture, media, parents, and their friends, among numerous other sources. In promoting meaningful discussions about relationships and sex education, students need to be aware of their own perspectives while also being prepared to engage in respectful dialogue with others about their unique perspectives. As a teacher, you of course also have your own unique perspective. However, your role as the teacher is to facilitate the students' perspectives while keeping within the boundaries established in this book.

KEY POINTS

- The self is an abstract concept that has been investigated by many subject disciplines.
- It is important to help students develop their sense of self to provide a basis from which to establish meaningful healthy relationships.
- Each person has a unique self and it is important to recognise that each self is equally important irrespective of how a person identifies.

- The self can be damaged for a variety of reasons.
- The self-concept consists of a balance between the self-image and the ideal-self. If they are relatively in balance, a student will have higher self-esteem.
- Dialogue is important to understand the range of perspectives.
- The highest form of thinking is an individual who is committed to a perspective, yet respects other perspectives, while being open to evaluating new evidence and, from this, reconsidering their perspective.
- Teaching relationships and sex education is more than a checklist or a resource pack: it needs proper dialogue.
- Unicorns, chameleons, beetles and strawberries can all help to explain the sense of self.

LESSONS IN LOVE & UNDERSTANDING 1: UNDERSTANDING THE SELF

For the RSE teaching that we advocate, 4-year-olds can be included in the KS1 learning, and 17-year-olds can be included in the KS4 learning.

KS1 (AGE 5–7 YEARS)

- Use one of the books in the recommended reading to introduce other perspectives.
- After reading the books, a simple discussion on other people's perspectives could be facilitated.
- Take the students for a walk with a mirror which they hold just below their eyes. It would be useful for one student to guide the other so that the other person does not walk into walls, trees, trip over obstacles, etc. The walk can be conducted both inside the school and outside. Then discuss what they preferred and why. This will enable them to look upwards, such as at the underside of trees in a park, etc. Again, discuss how we can see the world in different ways. (Note that this works effectively with any year group in KS1/2.)
- Play different pieces of music and discuss what pictures come up in students' minds, valuing the contribution of each.

(Continued)

- Use toys such as kaleidoscopes, 'bug-eye' viewers or prisms to change their perspective on how they see things. (Again, this works well for all year groups in primary.)
- Encourage the students to consider their identity by relating to their experience – for example, their class, their school, their name, their hobbies, etc.

KS2 (AGE 7–11 YEARS)

- The range of books identified in the resources section are all useful for introducing and discussing perspectives.
- Encourage the students to take a toy home for the weekend. We have used a bag of smoothed pebbles (available from most garden shops) and stick-on eyes (available from the internet) for this purpose. The students can then write an extract about the experience their toy has had, the things they have seen, and so forth.
- In art, the use of optical illusions could be explored. M.C. Escher's work is fantastic to use for perspective and could be used as a prompt for a story, especially his work such as 'Relativity' or 'Belvedere'.
- Further discussion could be elicited from many guided reading books, but also through discussing news or political events.
- An exercise in enabling the students to think about who they are is to take a photo of each student's face, then cut each photo in half. Each student sticks their photo on a sheet of paper and draws the other side of their head, but rather than adding their facial features, they draw pictures that represent them. A similar idea is for the students to use a shield template that they design to illustrate who they are.

KS3 (AGE 11–14 YEARS)

- As with the previous Key Stages, different books could be used to elicit discussion on perspective.
- Discuss the following quote: 'Many of the truths we cling to depend greatly on our own point of view.' (Obi Wan Kenobi, *Return of the Jedi*). To what extent do students agree with this quote? Can they think of examples where this is true?

- Encourage the students to draw timelines of their life, the significant moments, their best memories. Ask them to extend this into the future to consider where they would like to proceed.
- Discuss the role of the 'self' in the physical world and the virtual world. Do they have specific avatars? Why did they choose these? Do they behave differently in the real versus the virtual world? Do they think that celebrities are the same in the physical and virtual world?
- Introduce philosophical thought experiments. A good source is *The Pig That Wants to be Eaten* by Julian Baggini.

KS4 (AGE 14–16 YEARS)

- Further discussion could be developed about individual identity in the real and the virtual world.
- Use further thought experiments or moral paradoxes to help understand perspective.
- Draw a radar chart and encourage the students to list independent characteristics important to them (such as academic subjects, hobbies, interests, and so on). Ask them to evaluate where they are on each axis and whether any of these are out of kilter with what they are planning to do in the future.
- Invite the person responsible for careers to come in and talk about future study options. They may have access to questionnaires that enable the students to consider their strengths and possible future career options.
- Identify a current political debate. Set the students into groups to identify how different media cover the political angles, such as newspapers, television, social media, and so forth.

ADDITIONAL READING

KS1 (AGE 5–7 YEARS)

- *It's Okay To Be Different* by Todd Parr.
- *This is How We Do It: One Day in the Lives of Seven Kids from around the World* by Matt LaMothe.
- *Thunder Boy Jr.* by Sherman Alexie.
- *I Am Enough* by Grace Byers.

- *Superheroes Are Everywhere* by Kamala Harris.
- *Remarkably You* by Pat Zietlow Miller.

KS2 (AGE 7–11 YEARS)

- *Under My Hijab* by Hena Khan.
- *Step Into Your Power: 23 Lessons on How to Live Your Best Life* by Jamia Wilson.

KS3/4 (AGE 11–16 YEARS)

- *Mind Your Head* by Juno Dawson and Olivia Hewitt.
- *You're Not Lost: An Inspired Action Plan for Finding Your Own Way* by Maxie McCoy.

ADULTS

- *How To Talk So Kids Will Listen & Listen So Kids Will Talk* by Adele Faber and Elaine Mazlish.

2

GENDER

CONTENTS

CHAPTER OBJECTIVES

- To understand that gender is an expression of the self and part of an individual's personal identity.
- To recognise how gender has been traditionally assigned and the current influences on gender.
- To consider depression, dysmorphia and dysphoria in relation to gender.
- To appreciate that gender identity holds different levels of meaning and significance for different people.
- To consider four factors that teachers can use to support individuals.

WHY THIS CHAPTER?

We've designed this book so that you can read each chapter as a stand-alone guide. However, we will refer between different chapters as we go. You will soon get an idea of how we go about approaching each section, and key themes that encourage questioning, not making assumptions, inclusion and the promotion of love and respect. May we remind you of our earlier request for understanding and forgiveness. Throughout this book, you will often come across terms or statements that are problematic, in that they are not factually sound and can potentially cause offence because they don't reflect the truth for many people. Some of the terminology is dated, or has changed in meaning over time, and will continue to do so, so this is our disclaimer for what might not be politically correct but is written for the purpose of promoting mutual conceptual understanding. Our desire is to create as safe a space as possible in our relationship with you, the reader, so we hope not to be clumsy in our language, and to make this a relaxed and fun experience for us all.

The **LGBT** acronym (Lesbian, Gay, Bisexual, Transgender) and the associated rainbow flag are so well known that they even have their own emoji. Some of us are aware of the further extended versions such as **LGBTQI**+ or LGBTIQQ2A (with the addition of Intersex, Queer, **Questioning**, **two-spirited** and Allies). However, this still excludes other 'labels' such as pansexual and **asexual**, among others, and we dare say that such acronyms will continually evolve. To be honest, you could take all 26 letters of the alphabet, the digits 0 to 9, and any symbol, sequencing them in whatever order you wish because ultimately you are just you: a perfect and unique expression of your 'self'. The intent of using half the alphabet is to give a message of inclusion. However, when this lengthy acronym is met with confusion, it risks having the opposite effect. People can easily become alienated through feeling they cannot understand and that therefore this does not relate to them. We are here to unpack the jargon and take a closer look at this. Having started with the self (Chapter 1), let's now take a closer look at the labels we create as a society and how we make sense of them in the real world.

GENDER 101

The impact of gender as a biopsychosocial construct exists from the point of being a foetus in the womb, when parents hold curiosity around their child being male or female, sometimes enough to pay for early gender scans to inform them of whether they are *expecting* a girl or a boy. For most parents, this expectation is loaded with assumptions around the perceived stereotypical differences between girls and boys, and what one might hope for the future. From the point of birth, we are enveloped with the hopes, dreams and fantasy of what society has conjured up for us. Cheers, world!

INTERSEX/DSD

Back in reality, as many as one in every 1,500 babies are born with genitals that cannot be classified as male or female. This is an expert estimate, as Government agencies do not currently collect information about individuals with Differences/Diversity of Sexual Development (**DSD**), but this is what some experts agree, as listed by the American Psychological Association (see the Glossary for some DSD definitions). Many people do not have a biologically **binary** male or female presentation, certainly in the case of people born with intersex conditions or Diversity of Sexual Development. And sometimes for those with or without DSD conditions, gender identified at birth (through visual examination of the genitalia) is not, in fact, the true gender that the child/adult comes to identify (please refer to a glossary of Diversity in Sexual Development terms in the box below).

EXAMPLES OF DIVERSITY IN SEXUAL DEVELOPMENT

- Androgen Insensitivity Syndrome (AIS): an intersex condition where the cell has a partial or complete inability to respond to androgen resulting in impairing or preventing the masculinisation of genitalia in the foetus and the onset of secondary sexual characteristics at puberty.
- CAFAB: an acronym for 'coercively assigned female at birth', where a baby, whose genitalia may not be considered explicitly male or female, is assigned a specific female gender.
- CAMAB: an acronym for 'coercively assigned male at birth', where a baby, whose genitalia may not be considered explicitly male or female, is assigned a specific male gender.
- IAFAB: intersex assigned female at birth.
- IAMAB: intersex assigned male at birth.
- Klinefelter syndrome: an intersex condition where a baby assigned male at birth is born with an extra X **chromosome** (XXY), which results in the typical level of **testosterone** not being produced.
- Rokitansky syndrome: when a baby is born with an underdeveloped womb, or without a womb, **cervix** and upper **vagina** but does have ovaries.
- Turner syndrome: an intersex, genetic disorder affecting one in 2,000 babies assigned female at birth and have only one X chromosome. The effect of this is that the person may have shorter than average height or have underdeveloped ovaries.

Stonewall (2019a) predict that currently over 1% of the British population identify as **trans**. However, more specific statistics are provided later. Are you puzzled or surprised? What we are saying is that we continue, as a global society, to hold a whole range of assumptions and ideals on a newborn (sometimes unborn) baby, based on assigning gender at birth, by having a quick look at genitals, even though we know that – *news flash* – genitalia is *not* a reliable gender indicator! We know this biologically, psychologically, and sociologically, if you don't believe us. What you do or don't have, now or historically, between your legs, does not define you nor your gender identity – not in reality. Now, that leaves the job of us telling the rest – but isn't this kind of mission part of why you became a teacher? Unveil the truth, teach real life. You can do this!

BODY IMAGE

Body image in the ever-changing and developing human is always going to come with its challenges. For many people, the transforming body is a cause of varying degrees of psychological, and sometimes physiological, pain. This is something that we have always acknowledged in educating young people about puberty. Nobody ever said puberty was fun. However, what society and education has not focused on is when the psychological pain experienced is beyond that which we might find a typical emotional response to puberty. Teachers and parents are going to be key in noticing signs of distress that indicate the need for intervention and possibly GP referral to ensure that the right professional support is put in place. Consider the three Ds – depression, **dysmorphia** and dysphoria. Before we look at these in further depth, let's consider our societal taboos and the culture of 'things one does not talk about'. Death and sex are pretty high up there, along with mental health as a whole. So, the three Ds are often very well hidden. If we can create a safe space in which our young people can come to acknowledge and understand their own feelings, we are providing a rich and liberating education. The relationship between body and mind is a complex one, and if someone is experiencing conflict with the body they inhabit before puberty, it is unlikely that things will improve when they develop into an adult version of that same body.

DEPRESSION

Depression is an umbrella term that holds many different meanings. This can be useful as it requires a personalisation in order to understand what any one person is experiencing within this label. Although a psychological condition, secondary physiological symptoms of depression can be seen in various ways, from neglect of self-care, hygiene and health to self-harm and eating-disordered behaviours. Again, we must be cautious of pathologising where we can support young people in understanding the psychology behind the behaviour, and where we can educate on all the various ways, shapes and forms that constitute 'normal'. The trick is to open up conversations. Let's stop hiding away from difficult and emotive topics. Antoni's voice shows us how vital this communication can be:

> Not being able to talk to anyone really damaged me. It was only when I was very close to suicide did I know I needed help. The last person I ever thought I would disclose to was a **cis**-male who was a mental health gateway worker, working partly at the school I attended. He put me in touch with a **Gender Identity Clinic** which has been incredible. Being able to speak to someone about how I felt all through my life was a real sense of release in appreciating that 'it's not just me'. I felt that there were people who actually understood and supported people like me. It was the **hormones** which had the most remarkable impact. I had been on antidepressants following my close call to ending things, yet the hormone prescription gave me a sense of balance between my mind and my body. Almost overnight the depression had gone. (Antoni, age 28)

Talking about suicide does not make people want to kill themselves, but it does reduce the stress and isolation for somebody already thinking about it. We must teach that there is help and support right here, right now, and it starts with us. Never underestimate the power of showing that you care and you want to help. Too often, we signpost students and colleagues to somebody we deem to be the more appropriate professional, as we feel unequipped to effectively manage mental health issues. This message can be damaging to a young person already feeling marginalised, isolated or overwhelmed, to sense that their trusted adult echoes these feelings in being unable to hold, contain or sit with what the young person chooses to share (i.e. their life). Of course, it's important to make the appropriate referrals and seek specialist support where possible (see Chapter 8 for guidance and signposting). However, as teacher, educator, parent or guardian, there is so much you can offer by being there to listen and offering your support. In Chapter 7, we help you structure a peer supervision group, in order to look after yourself in the process of supporting learners.

BODY DYSMORPHIA

Body dysmorphia can be experienced by individuals who do not necessarily have **Body Dysmorphic Disorder**. Social media, the pornography industry and the world of cosmetically altered celebrities all contribute to young people feeling that their bodies are flawed in comparison to the air-brushed, silicone enhanced, anally bleached images that surround them in Western culture. Dysmorphia becomes pathologised when behaviours become obsessive and problematic in an attempt to manage distress caused by the perceived flaw. Common gender stereotypes affect perception – for example, males are more likely to fixate around feeling they are not tall enough, or have large enough hands, feet or penises. Females are more likely to see themselves as too fat, too tall, or their facial features too '**masculine**'. Interestingly, when we look at eating disorder studies, research has found that trans females and cis-females show the same patterns and prominence in anorexia and bulimia, indicating a clear link between gender ideation and body dysmorphia (Witcomb et al., 2015).

GENDER DYSPHORIA

As with depression and dysmorphia, **gender dysphoria** is something that can be experienced to various levels and not solely by people who wish to **transition**. As 'homosexuality' was originally classified as a mental illness, so too was gender dysphoria. Fortunately, we gained a little wisdom around sexuality and gender over the past decade (see Chapter 5). Identifying as gay or trans (even both at the same time) is not a disorder, and not all people who identify as transgender seek any clinical intervention as such. However, for those who experience severe dysphoria, they often are recommended **hormone therapy** in order to find gender comfort: to help bring body and mind to balance. For some, surgeries are required in order to achieve relief from the dysphoria, but even beyond transition, it is possible that the individual will still experience symptoms of dysphoria and/or dysmorphia due to things such as fertility, height, frame, body hair and various features that we have a set of assumptions for based on our biopsychosocially constructed gender dichotomy, and what we have come to associate as masculine or **feminine**. Masculine: tall, broad muscular build, strong body, facial hair, strong brow and jaw line, prominent Adam's apple, large hands, feet and penis – all in working order, **erection**, ejaculation and sperm count ready (any time) for reproduction. Feminine: petite, slim, pretty, long hair, no body hair or facial hair, small hands, feet and waist, pert breasts in proportion to waist/height (like a Barbie doll), designer vagina. Ability (and desire) to conceive and carry a baby. Let's introduce some adolescent voices in response to this:

> Looking back on it, puberty at school was just a really stressful time. All I can think of is *pressure*. Suddenly there was a pressure for shoulders to broaden, voice to break, balls to drop, **pubes** to grow . . . . In school there was just no hiding it, and that pressure extended into wearing the right clothes, listening to the right music and being seen to be the cool guy for all the right reasons . . . whatever those were. It was only on leaving school I felt I could be me. (Bruce, age 19)

Bruce is a cis-male teenager, who is not experiencing high levels of distress around puberty and would not be considered to have symptoms of depression, dysphoria or dysmorphia. We use his voice, as this tells us something of the everyday issues of gender expectations that affect adolescents. The gender assumptions and stereotypes that exist are not only problematic for trans people and those with intersex/DSD, they affect every single one of us, on so many levels. This is far from ideal for healthy child development, and this problem continues beyond adolescence and into adulthood, influencing ideas around professional skills, talent sets, social skills, academic ability, and so on. Look at the list in Table 2.1 and answer Male, Female or **Non-binary** for the group you would think society regarded as the strongest in the particular category.

Who does society believe to be best at the following? Pick just one category without stopping to think too much.

Table 2.1   Who does society believe to be best at the following?

Skill, talent, ability	Male	Female	Non-binary
Midwifery and nursing			
IT project management			
Multi-tasking			
Playing and coaching football			
Driving and manoeuvring large vehicles			
Hair-design and make-up artistry			
Playing drums in a band			
Putting the bins out			
Gaining the highest turnover in the world of business			
Child-care and babysitting			

   This can be an interesting exercise in considering where these notions come from, and how many of them you have subconsciously absorbed as truths, without having questioned your reasoning. Applied to classroom teaching, we can consider some of the classic assumptions – for example, play and (the now generally debunked concept of) preferred learning style, as both have had long associations and commonalities assumed to belong to boys or girls. Indeed, you might think, 'Well, actually – I *do* tend to find that the girls in my class gravitate towards creative group play and interactions, and the boys towards more active and less structured play'. We accept that this may often be the case, but not *always*, and even for those who follow the *typical* pattern, this could well be nurture rather than nature, as after all, society has programmed us from before birth.

   The reason that gender takes a prominent position in this book is because these same themes will run through every chapter and lesson. Our biopsychosocial constructs affect the way the world is today, and we will see later in Chapters 5 and 6 how history, law and policy has shaped this. First, though, let's stop and think again. We invite you to take some time to consider your own gender identity. What does your own gender identity mean to you? Perhaps you label yourself (e.g. non-binary, gender queer, male, female). Does this fit with the messages you have received from around you (family, education, media, etc.)? Most of us will experience some degree of conflict within the **gender role** we identify with and whether we entirely fit with the associated norms for this cohort. This might not be constant throughout one's life. This may be experienced during significant chronological/biological stages of development. For example, popular culture describes as tomboys and ladettes infant/young girls that show a preference for activities considered to be boys' interests, and perhaps even older teenage females who present themselves in a certain dress, behaviour and manner. We commonly hear how men feel 'emasculated' should they suffer fertility problems, and particularly erectile dysfunction. And the hormone shifts at both puberty, and again in menopause and **andropause** are all associated with mood swings and irritability among many other unpleasant experiences affecting general well-being. So, we have a complex mix of things going on here and variation in how any individual experiences such events. Yet, we continue to generalise and hold tight, as a society, to the constructs we have created that make us all feel inadequate throughout every stage of life.

> It's everywhere: a system of thought and a set of inverted and discriminatory practices in our laws, culture and economy that feminists call the patriarchy. Feminists are not out to get us. They are out to get the patriarchy. (Webb, 2017, pp. 237–8)

As Robert Webb so brilliantly puts it in *How Not To Be a Boy*, this is the case for *everyone*, very much including cisgender (those who identify as the gender they were assigned at birth) people. For many unborn babies, they already have a whole set of pink floral clothes and nursery to match – or boyish-style blues and reds wardrobe, furnishings and accessories – according to the genitalia a scan picture showed. The more thrifty parents choose white or neutral colours 'in case the opposite sex comes next' because we all know that newborns have strong opinions on colour schemes and would be mortified to be seen in the wrong colour for their gender cohort! The parent or parents and wider family of the unborn child may also fall into the roles expected of their gender. In Western culture, stereotypically, granny knits or helps to prepare for comfort and nurture, and grandad builds the cot and does the 'more manly and practical DIY jobs'. There are pressures and conceived ideas on how one gives birth (no unnatural interventions and pretend not to feel the pain, female), what happens immediately after birth (if there is a father figure present, he has defined roles to play, as do matriarchal grandparents), and that's before the child is even 24 hours into the world. By that stage, too, most parents have had to make a decision about maternity/paternity leave, who is going to be 'the main caregiver', and who might be the person to pursue a career and be the family 'breadwinner', and so it begins, again and again as we continue to repeat history.

GENDER INFLUENCES

Whether the education you are providing is as a parent or a professional, and either in a home, community or school learning environment, you will be aware of the influences everywhere that tell us what being male or female means. If you now consider the age/s and stage/s of the young person whose education you influence, you will be aware of the messaging about gender *conformity* that we all receive through our entire lives, everywhere we go. There is almost no escape. However, you can have a massive impact on this by the learning environment that you create. This is a great challenge, and, rather than making this stressful, it might be viewed as an exercise in mindfulness. It is about rethinking the ways things are in your learning environment. Are there equal opportunities for everybody to explore, create and learn in an expressive way? What gender roles are represented in the learning literature library? Look for subtle messaging on things like wall posters, or even the way in which you group pupils/students or segregate them for use of toilet cubicles. Let's challenge ourselves and ask, 'Is this in the best interest of the child/students?'. There may be spiritual or religious beliefs that lead to certain decisions where gender divides are custom and important to the faith group that put them in place. Of course, there are reasons why we might have certain interpretations and reasons for decisions made that discriminate against young people of a particular gender cohort, such as medical grounds. As applies throughout this book, what we ask is that you mindfully consider improvements to the best of your ability, in the spirit of equality and inclusion for all. Doing so is an act of love and excellent modelling for those you educate.

All of us are restricted by biopsychosocial gender constructions, and particularly our trans communities. Please see the Glossary for the full definition of how we are using *trans* and *transition* here and note that when any gender labels – such as female, male or non-binary – are used, this may or may not refer to somebody with a trans history. We use *trans* to describe somebody who is at any point of transition, from the point of self-recognition of gender identity other to the one that was assigned at birth, to the point at which that individual finds gender comfort. It is possible to have more than one transition phase over a lifetime, as we have recognised, and that how a person identifies with gender (and sexuality, Chapter 3) is not fixed through their natural human development. As with cisgender people, trans people are victims of our gender-stereotyped world. Over the past ten years there has been a shift in how the World Professional Association of Transgender Health has viewed transition and the binary way of viewing 'a transition goal towards female or male' has made way for the goal of health being based on finding gender identity congruence or comfort. This means that there is expert recognition for non-binary gender identities, which is great news for human rights and an important step towards equality. Please see the Glossary for some of the many ways in which people might categorise or label their gender identity. Remain mindful, though, that those labels mean different things to the people who choose to use them, and many do not choose to label themselves at all.

With all of this in mind, let's recap on what we have learnt earlier, and then we will offer some practical advice. Let's think again about gender definitions.

HISTORY

Interpreted from the earliest recordings in Western culture, we are taught that there are two genders – male and female. The Bible says that God created human beings of male and female sex. However, there is no direct mention of gender. There are also many biblical examples of gender variations in breaking with stereotypes – for example, Jacob and his twin brother Esau who are described in roles of male and female dichotomy. There are also several females in *non-conforming* roles: Deborah, the judge, Euhodia and Syntyche, the preachers, and so on.

BIOLOGY

When a baby is born, gender is assigned by visual inspection of the genitalia. This is proven to be scientifically inaccurate when we consider babies born with intersex conditions or DSD. We also know that 1% of the population identify as trans. Here we have scientific and medical evidence that this system of determining gender is invalid.

PSYCHOLOGY

By pathologising those who do not *conform* to a male/female gender dichotomy, we create within society an unnatural way of relating to others, as the true self is repressed and the natural feelings that the individual is experiencing are weighted with shame, guilt and the feeling of being abnormal and unworthy of love. These feelings are damaging to the psyche, and, understandably, can lead to low self-esteem, loneliness, isolation, depression and anxiety. The circumstantial responses of these types of psychological issues, in response to society's prejudice (this predicament is sometimes referred to as *minority stress*), can lead to further pathologising as the individual is viewed as **'gender non-conforming'**, as well as showing comorbidity with other psychiatric disorders. For example, during transition, somebody with gender dysphoria may feel depressed and anxious as a result of this process and the associated stresses. It does not mean that the person is mentally ill or suffering clinical depression or anxiety, much like anybody going through a huge life-changing event such as relationship changes or bereavement. There are certain moods and psychological states one would expect as normal and healthy responses to very challenging life circumstances.

SOCIOLOGY

In 2020, the world still largely attempts to squeeze into heteronormative family systems, whereby idealistic goals are revered: cis-female and cis-male, in monogamous heterosexual relationships, often within the same culture or faith group, and certainly sharing the same 'feminine' and 'masculine' binary stereotypical traits as those within their gender cohort, raising a child in keeping with this pattern in the family system. In reality, family systems do not operate like this and as a society this template does not work (see Chapter 3 for greater detail).

CULTURAL ANTHROPOLOGY

Our own experience may be of a binary society, yet many cultures have recognised that gender is multifaceted. For example, Western anthropologists identified the **berdache** in Native American tribes, such as the **nádleehi** from Navaho/Navajo culture, physical males with combined elements of both male and female spirit, and as such were held in high regard due to their close alignment in mediating between the physical and spiritual planes of existence. The *acault* from Myanmar were similarly respected, in that such feminine males were possessed, then married to *Manguedon*, the female spirit of good fortune and success. From the *maa khii* in northern Thailand, the ***calabai/calaalai*** in Indonesia, the ***fa'afafine*** from Samoan culture, through to the six genders recognised in Judaism (such as the Zachar, Nekevah, Androgynos, Tumtum, Ay'lonit and Saris). Indeed, all of these cultures and religions highlight that such genders were considered spiritually advanced, so much so that often they were deemed their spiritual leaders. Many of the terms have been considered derogatory and have subsequently been replaced with the general term 'two-spirit' since the early 1990s, although this term is also seen as contentious as it is a Western interpretation for non-Western cultures.

TRANS KIDS IN THE UK

In British schools, we have seen a dramatic rise in the number of children and young people who identify as trans, gender queer, non-binary, or one of the many other gender-type labels that we have provided at the end of this chapter, so you can familiarise yourself with these terms. The British Social Attitudes Survey (Curtice et al., 2019) has highlighted that trans people and their stories are becoming increasingly visible, possibly as a result of high-profile media cases such as Caitlyn Jenner, Chelsea Manning and Laverne Cox. There are seven adult Gender Identity Clinics (GIC) in the UK, and the Gender Identity Development Service (GIDS) is the paediatric service that operates from three of those centres (London, Exeter and Leeds, when we went to print). From GIDS data, there has been a 2,500% increase in referrals since 2009–10 to 2,590 children in the year 2018–19 (for adults there has been a 240% increase). As we have outlined in the Introduction, Stonewall have suggested that 1% of the UK population identify as trans, with other sources indicating a similar number – for example, there are estimates of between 0.17 to 1.3% of adolescents from a study by Connolly et al. (2016), through to 1.3% of 16 to 19 years olds (Sumia et al., 2017). Population surveys in the USA indicate that 0.5% of the population identity as transgender (Crissman et al., 2017). The Government Equalities Office (2018) suggest that there are as many as 200,000 to 500,000 trans people in the UK. However, they assert that there is no robust data, and there is a call for gender identity to be included in the 2021 Census. The data presented here indicates a conservative estimate of 0.5% of people identifying as trans, through to a more liberal 1%, which means that in a 1,000 student school there could be five to ten students with gender dysphoria. Even if there is one student in your school, your understanding and intervention could help change a life, perhaps even save a life, given that one in four (27%) of children and young people who identify as trans have attempted suicide, 72% have self-harmed at least once, and nine in ten (89%) have experienced suicidal ideation (Stonewall, 2019b).

Not all of these children and young people seek any kind of support or medical intervention, although clearly with increased social awareness, we are enabling people to step forward and be counted in the way they personally identify. In theory, it is fantastic that we have reached this level of liberation. However, as this book goes to print, the challenges faced by people in the UK experiencing gender dysphoria and trans people who seek psychological support and/or medical/surgical intervention are huge, with waiting lists that are several years long to access the care they need through the NHS. This is a national crisis that puts gender patients at great risk of mental health deterioration and suicide. As places of education and educators we must consider this in representation and provision within our professional field. In this section, we will provide you with some background for understanding trans matters that may come up for pupils, families and staff at school, and suggestions of ways in which you can offer support. We will also outline ways in which you can include teaching on transgender health and well-being as part of RSE.

Let's begin by hearing the voice of PJ, who identifies as a 10-year-old trans-boy, and his teacher Ms Q, who identifies as a 46-year-old cis-female.

PJ: I just get really really annoyed when people 'she' me, and then I don't want to speak. It's getting worse as I grow up 'cos people think I've got a high voice, or they try and put me into girl groups for sport. Stuff like that. I'm with GIDS now, and my family are going to the groups they run for parents who are worried about their trans kids, and we meet with some other families like us. I want to start T before I have periods and grow a body that I don't want then need top-surgery. My doctor at GIDS says I'm too young to start T but is thinking about **blockers** . . .

Ms Q: Hang on, PJ, I'm losing you – can you explain a bit? I understand it's upsetting if people misgender you, and I'm really glad you have support from the Gender Identity Development Service – that sounds helpful. What are T and blockers?

PJ: Hormones, testosterone. And blockers are the ones that will stop me having a girl puberty – they block the girl hormones. My appointments are just taking ages and all the time I'm worried I'm becoming more like a girl [cries]. I don't want to come to school like this. I don't want to leave my house at all.

PJ is in a difficult predicament because there are many health factors that need to be weighed up by the specialist paediatricians working in gender care. Currently, in the UK *cross-hormone treatment* is not offered at NHS children's services, and a patient must wait until they are transferred to adult services and are approaching 18 years old. There are a number of obstacles that might add to the feelings of distress faced by trans children and young people looking for gender treatments such as hormone therapy and surgical interventions, listed below:

- Coming out: it is often difficult for young children to be taken seriously if they are experiencing gender discomfort, as it is a tricky thing to verbalise and not necessarily noticeable to anybody around them as to the cause of their distress.

- Parental control: once recognised by parents/carers, it is natural that most try to make things easier for their child, perhaps by being more sensitive to distressing factors and allowing autonomy over things like activity choice, gender of playmates, clothing items and hairstyle, hoping that this phase will pass when the child feels happier. Some parents come to realise and support a child with their gender concerns, but some will not and this can leave the child powerless to seek help (unless school becomes aware and offers support).

- Accessing professional support: although every step is taken so that young people access NHS care as quickly as possible, there are long waiting lists at paediatric gender services in the UK. It is not simple for a young person to get a referral and then there is a waiting list at every stage (psychological assessment, counselling therapy, specialist recommendation, endocrinology, referral to adult services, and so on).

- Due to this situation, there is a reliance on partnership between Child and Adolescent Mental Health Services (CAMHS), school and GP to support young people and their families suffering distress around their gender identity. CAMHS are already under huge amounts of strain and as an organisation they have no more gender identity training and expertise than teachers and GPs do. At the time this book went to print, we were not aware of any teacher training courses, nor any medical schools that were offering specific Gender Identity training as part of general medicine studies in the UK. So this isn't really what you can call a support network.

- Once a child eventually does make it to referral and through to the first specialist gender identity clinic appointment, they usually find this very difficult, as there still appears to be no help – just a very long list of questions for assessment purposes and occasional support networks. What tends to happen is that families and young people who are willing and able to engage set up their own social networks with people they meet connected to their clinic, or to one of the supporting advocacy charities such as Mermaids (more about resources in Chapter 6).
- Of course, not all children and young people will be supported by their families, especially if they are attending clinics, and attending a support group means travel costs and time out of education. This situation can create even greater tension and distress for the young person and their family.
- If it is decided that a young person should have hormone blockers, this is not a decision to be taken lightly, as the blockers prevent normal development of secondary sex characteristics, such as bone growth and brain maturation, until either blockers are stopped or cross-hormone therapy begins, in which case the young person then begins puberty with hormone therapy that corrects the balance according to their needs as assessed by the paediatric endocrinologist. There is also the matter of future family planning (this can be a very hard thing to anticipate or think about for anyone under 18, and especially with gender concerns at the forefront of their minds). **Gamete storage** is greatly encouraged before hormone therapy begins, although this comes with its own set of challenges and costs.
- By the time a young person is at this stage and has managed to get a place at adult services (another long wait) they are, unsurprisingly, often at their wits end, and their families', too. By the age of 18 they could have been psychologically waiting (from the time they've identified as trans) for the treatment they need for well over a decade, then to be told that there are many more years to wait if they are to require surgeries for **vaginoplasty/phalloplasty**, etc.

This is absolutely not a dig at the NHS or any of the gender clinics in the UK; they are wonderful centres full of hard-working, highly skilled and compassionate clinicians. They are simply victims of the huge demand that has occurred over the last decade and which continues to grow. Between 2010 and 2017, GIDS in the UK saw a 2,000% increase in referrals. Many UK private gender identity clinics also had waiting lists as this book went to print. This truly is a national crisis and another issue that schools are trying to manage, with no training or support to do so. Yet, the fact that the Department for Education has written a new policy on RSE 2020 means that there is an acknowledgement for the need to include transgender health education, and from this small seed, schools will take this forward while finding innovative ways to champion and celebrate gender diversity. Schools are fundamental in changing society: just think of how Greta Thunberg has revolutionised thinking on climate change.

Some of the people experiencing severe minority stress, exacerbated by barriers preventing appropriate access to care, are your students, pupils and family members. Some of them are your colleagues, friends and neighbours. Outside of the UK and across the world, there are different healthcare systems, politics, cultures and socioeconomic factors that will similarly impact on the stress experienced by people of all ages, backgrounds, cultures and creeds. In many countries in the world, it is simply too dangerous to transition in any way, as the penalty would be ostracisation from the community, and assault, torture and murder are very real threats. Life or death suddenly makes your job as an educator take on a whole new level of significance – we're sure you agree. You can help this situation in several ways.

THE ROLE OF EDUCATION

Education, on various levels, is absolutely key to making the world a better place to live, for everybody. Starting from the age and stage of having a concept of family and community relationships, an infant should understand that people are all different, unique beings. Should gender matter? You may be thinking of families you know or have become aware of through the media who chose to raise a child **gender neutral**. One might wonder how on earth this was possible without screening the child from the outside world, or what the effects on social interactions might be for a child raised as such among peers who are not raised in this way. It does pose some interesting questions, and there has been much media discussion and debate on the topic. However, the idea of the entire abolition of gender identities – which would be one strategy in addressing the biopsychosocial paradigms in which we all find ourselves – would also fail to allow individuals to connect with parts of their unique identity that feel fitting to them. For example, we authors both have family members who fought hard to strive for their unique version of gender identity against the social and professional expectations of their generation. One male relative became a successful academic despite the battles of gender dysphoria, transition and chronic, debilitating illness. This courageous gentleman overcame adversity, winning battles over mind, body and soul to achieve his full potential in his tragically shortened life. Education, and furthering the education of others, continues to be a noble focus for those who truly have to question the meaning of life and the legacy or impact they wish to leave for future generations. The other family member was one of the first ever female first-class honours graduates in Maths and Physics, before becoming a university lecturer of Maths, then Head of Mathematics at a Scottish secondary school. She was also originally from an immigrant family and had to learn very quickly to speak Scottish English at primary school due to her wartime fear that her family would be deported as suspected spies. In 2020, UK schools are still striving to bring female pupils in line with males in Maths and Science, so this is a celebration of equality and overcoming adversity, and we must champion the exceptions to our societal constructs in order to move forward and be the best version of our true selves we can be. Historical, political and many other reasons (see more in Chapter 5) might make one very protective of preserving certain labels of belonging. Connecting with others through shared features of and belonging to a group identity is how communities are made. What we are *not* trying to achieve is taking belonging and identity away from anybody – quite the opposite. So, here is a step-by-step guide to what that might look like for you as an educator.

1. **Make no assumptions** Even if it is your own offspring that you are educating, don't assume that you know how they feel in terms of their gender identity. How a person feels about their gender identity can shift over time. The experience of feeling pressure from media to look and dress in certain ways, or feelings of not belonging in their gender assigned at birth, as well as feeling established in

consistency in presenting in a certain way over a certain duration, are all common and normal experiences within child development and adolescence, and can occur at any time. Sometimes a young person is waiting for the right time to share their feelings.

In terms of making assumptions about pupils or students who are not known to you, don't assume their gender identity by their clothing, style, behaviour or appearance. As you look at the style of young people and students, when they are making decisions on their own clothing, very often styling is gender neutral. T-shirts, hoodies, sweatshirts, jeans and unisex footwear have been the universal uniform of adolescents of all genders for decades. Unless by style choice, why would a trans or gender queer kid choose a pink frock, a blue three-piece suit and moustache, or a cross between the two, in the hope that a stranger might get their pronouns right? Hair is also so varied in style and length for that age group that you cannot expect any visual cues.

2. **Inclusive administration systems and facilities** Let's avoid unnecessarily awkward and potentially embarrassing moments. Form filling has been a widely discussed subject among trans support groups. However, many organisations have improved their approach to this area, and as authors we have been pleasantly surprised to be asked in public places such as libraries and GP surgeries for gender identity and preferred title and pronouns. If your place of work or organisations you belong to have not already updated their systems to provide those options, this is a great start in developing an inclusion policy (more in Chapter 6). The preference would be to have the option to write a gender or sexuality identity in if one wishes, rather than to have to tick boxes, in which the option of 'other' can add to feelings of isolation for those who don't identify in the named categories, or who don't necessarily want to disclose such information, finding it to be irrelevant.

A space for preferred name on forms is also massively useful. Many schools use children's nicknames when it is stated that this is 'preferred'. Being called by a name that is comfortable is important for all of us as human beings. It's a simple token of respect to ask for, and one that gives autonomy in a world where very often children and young people feel powerless. Adults tend to slip up with name and pronoun changes far more than children and young people who adapt to any name change. It's okay to make mistakes. Apologise, move on and try harder for next time to remember, even if that means writing yourself a prompt.

Toilets and changing facilities are another area that can easily be managed in a way that is comfortable for everybody. Most people do not have gendered toilets in their homes, so why on earth would we have them anywhere else? Most modern sports changing facilities are unisex. But for those that are not, if your toilet cubicles are *not* labelled 'Male/female' and instead just labelled 'toilet', at least there is an option for anybody, for whatever reason, that does not wish to publicly change clothing/be naked in a shared gender-specific changing area. Expecting people with gender dysphoria to use the accessible toilet cubicles/restrooms is not an acceptable alternative, especially for a person who does not require supported access due to illness, disability or special needs. This is also depriving somebody who requires that accessible toilet from using it. These kinds of changes just require some common sense to be applied. Don't forget that such changes also apply for the staff team as well as the students.

3. **You can help** If anybody should trust you with their feelings around their gender identity, remember that it is an honour to be that trusted person. Remember that this is not necessarily a *problem* for them, though, and should not be treated or regarded as such. As with any personal sharing, a helpful response would be to thank the person for sharing with you and to ask if there is anything that you/the school might be able to do in support. (There is further guidance on this when looking at building policy in Chapter 6.) Now you are aware of some of the gender issues that affect all of us, you may become more tuned in when, for example, a student has potential in an area of education that they are reluctant to pursue due to perceived gender norms from society and their peers. For example, school sports clubs can actively encourage all inclusion by holding unisex groups. If you are in a school where you notice male staff are teaching rugby and football, and females are netball and cheerleading, mix it up. What a great way to improve your own skill set and be a healthy role model.

CONCLUSION

This chapter has explored the concept of gender as a biopsychosocial construct and the many assumptions that have infiltrated society to affect the way in which humans live and the roles we play, as individuals, and as families and communities, from the time of conception, throughout life to death. We have considered various versions of normal development and how gender impacts on the challenges of puberty and adolescence that directly affect our learners. Depression, dysphoria and dysmorphia are introduced as symptoms to be aware of in students who are experiencing high levels of distress in relation to body, mind and self-perception as influenced by society and the notion of gender *conformity*. This chapter provides guidance for a whole-school approach to integrating equal opportunities for all genders, and then looks at the situation for young people in the UK who identify as trans, and how educators can actively support them. The chapter asks the educator to consider their own stance and ideas around gender in order to have an enriched understanding of the topic, so as to provide students with a healthy comprehension of gender, which will be imbedded in how education is provided, at all levels and within all classes, as well as being explicitly taught in RSE.

KEY POINTS

- Gender is an expression of the self and part of an individual's personal identity.
- Gender has traditionally been assigned through examining genitalia at birth; however, there are numerous components of gender.
- How depression, dysmorphia and dysphoria occur in relation to gender.
- As teachers, there are simple ways to support a student identifying with gender concerns: make no assumptions, develop inclusive systems and facilities, appreciate that you can help, and develop a robust education on gender and sexuality through RSE.

LESSONS IN LOVE & UNDERSTANDING 2: GENDER

(For the RSE teaching that we advocate, 4-year-olds can be included in the KS1 learning and 17-year-olds can be included in the KS4 learning.)

KS1 (AGE 5–7 YEARS)

- Present a number of miniature objects/toys before a child/group/class and ask that they divide them into groups of FEMALE (girl) MALE (boy) EITHER (boy or girl) or NEITHER (not sure or not belonging to gender). Followed by group discussion about these ideas.
- Ask the class to draw a picture representing 'When I grow-up I would like to be . . . '. Once complete, celebrate these dreams and also ask if there are any other roles/jobs they would like to try and check if there are ideas of gender barriers in place – e.g. many KS1 children will only have experience of their parents, carers, health professionals, teachers and retail workers. The desire to be a firefighter or a soldier is often restricted to boys through media stereotyping, and the care professions (including teaching at KS1) restricted to girls through ratios within their experience.
- Create a list of rules for how to make life fairer for girls and boys. Perhaps you can present these verbally or as a wall display asking the child/children to ensure that the colours and presentation are appealing for everybody to listen to or look at/read.
- Source story-time literature exploring gender constructs (see recommended reading lists).

KS2 (AGE 7–11 YEARS)

- Draw a long line or arc representing a spectrum of gender, with MALE/MASCULINE at one end and FEMALE/FEMININE at the other end. Ask child/group of children to place inanimate objects or word cards onto the spectrum, with the option of not placing them on at all, to have a group conversation about our gender associations. There are no right or wrong answers, just lots of possibilities, and

(Continued)

this should be a fun activity to challenge everyone's perspectives and validate individuality.

- Run a biology lesson (visual resource suggested) presenting the differences in normal human bodies. Present the differences in shapes and sizes, colour, presentation of ageing, developing normal people, with an importance in representing female and male as not dependent on physical appearance; in fact, it is possible to be a female with two, one or no breasts, and a male with no penis, and it is also possible to feel no sense of belonging to either binary.
- Ask child/pairs/small groups to do some research in your place of learning, and create a proposal for how the school/community/world could be a fairer place for gender equality. This could be presented verbally or on wall displays, or even sent out online as a political statement.
- Source appropriate literature for exploring gender construct (see Additional reading).

KS3 (AGE 11–14 YEARS)

- Provide flip-chart paper, pens and varied craft supplies as available, and ask the young person/small group to create an image representing the perfect female. Once complete, provide the resources fresh and ask for an image representing the perfect male. Individuals/groups then provide feedback, and compare and contrast the qualities they have represented. Discuss and debate.
- Present on **gender variance** and the importance of showing respect to others, regardless of their similarities or differences in identity and presentation. Talk about the appropriate use of pronouns and not making assumptions. Ask students for a creative piece (poetry, prose, art, music) as an expression of gender equality.
- Understanding what being trans means and how to seek support for self or support others during transition and beyond.
- Source appropriate literature for exploring gender constructs (see recommended reading lists).

KS4 (AGE 14–16 YEARS)

- Divide the class into research groups and ask them to explore and present on some gender concepts of your choice – e.g. **feminism**, transition, the modern man, non-binary gender, etc.

- Hold a debate on the theme of gender equality.
- Teach a lesson on trans health providing sources of further information, support and encouraging students to look out for one another if they see signs of their friend's mental health declining.
- Source appropriate literature for exploring gender constructs (see Additional reading).

ADDITIONAL READING

KS1 (AGE 5–7 YEARS)

- *Pink Is for Boys* by Robb Pearlman.
- *Julian Is a Mermaid* by Jessica Love.
- *Dress Like a Girl* by Patricia Toht.
- *Don't Call Me Princess* by Kate Evans.

KS2 (AGE 7–11 YEARS)

- *The Boy in the Dress* by David Walliams.
- *Fearless Mary: Mary Fields, American Stagecoach Driver* by Tami Charles.
- *Stories for Boys Who Dare to be Different* (1 and 2) by Ben Brooks.
- *Good Night Stories For Rebel Girls* (1 and 2) by Elena Favilli and Francesca Cavallo.
- *Boys Who Made A Difference* by Michelle Roehm McCann.
- *Girls Who Rocked The World* by Michelle Roehm McCann.

KS3/4 (AGE 11–16 YEARS)

- *Trans Teen Survival Guide* by Owl and Fox Fisher.
- *Trans Mission: My Quest to a Beard* by Alex Bertie.
- *Not Just A Tomboy: A Trans Masculine Memoir* by Caspar J. Baldwin.
- *Yes, You Are Trans Enough: My Transition from Self-Loathing to Self-Love* by Mia Violet.
- *Manhood: The Bare Reality* by Laura Dodsworth.
- *Womanhood: The Bare Reality* by Laura Dodsworth.
- *Girl Activist* by Louisa Kamps.

ADULTS

- *How Not To Be A Boy* by Robert Webb.
- *How To Be Champion: My Autobiography* by Sarah Millican.
- *Manhood: The Bare Reality* by Laura Dodsworth.
- *Womanhood: The Bare Reality* by Laura Dodsworth.
- *You and Your Gender Identity: A Guide to Discovery* by Dara Hoffman-Fox.
- *Girl, Woman, Other* by Bernadine Evaristo.

Below are examples of gender identity labels to give an idea of some of the descriptive terms people use to help define their own gender identity.

Agender: A person who does not identify by gender and rejects the concept of gender for their own identity.

Androgyne: A person who is non-binary, identifying on the gender continuum as either both male and female, neither male nor female, or somewhere in between male and female stereotypical dichotomies.

Aporagender: A gender identity and a universal term for being a non-binary gender and still experiencing a strong sense of a specific gender that is neither male nor female in a binary sense.

Bigender: A person who has, or experiences, two genders.

Cis/cisgender: A person whose gender identity is the same as the sex and/or gender they were assigned at birth.

Demi-boy/demi-guy: Someone who partly identifies as male but not fully.

Demigender: A person who has or experiences a partial connection to one or more genders.

Demi-girl/demi-female: Someone who partly identifies as female but not fully.

Enby: This term is used to shorten 'non-binary' as 'NB' and is an identity term already claimed as meaning 'non-black', referring to race. However, some people identifying as non-binary use both or neither enby and NB.

Fem or femme: A shortened term for 'feminine', the gender expression, behaviour, dress and mannerisms traditionally associated with women.

Gender neutral: A person who identifies as having a gender that is neutral – neither exclusively female nor male.

Genderqueer: the term 'queer' is here reclaimed to celebrate a unique version of gender identity that lies outside of perceived gender norms.

Intergender: A person who identifies as a mix of binary genders.

Masc: A shortened term for 'masculine', the gender expression, behaviour, dress and mannerisms traditionally or stereotypically associated with men.

Maverique: A person who exists independent of male and female gender identity.

Maxigender: A person who experiences many, if not all, available genders.

Neutrois: A person whose gender is neutral.

Non-binary: A person who does not identify as having a binary gender or perhaps a gender at all.

Pangender: A person who experiences many, if not all, genders.

Transfeminine: A person assigned male at birth but who has, or expresses themselves in, a predominantly feminine manner.

Transmasculine: A person assigned female at birth but who has, or expresses themselves in, a predominantly masculine manner.

Trigender: A person who has or experiences three genders.

3

RELATIONSHIPS

CONTENTS

> **CHAPTER OBJECTIVES**
>
> - To understand the link between the self and relationships.
> - To critically consider what a 'norm' is.
> - To consider our responsibilities to the new generation in teaching about healthy relationships.
> - To appreciate the affect of cultural values on the developing student.
> - To understand the role of education in teaching about relationships.
> - To consider appropriate representation and inclusion of all groups when teaching about relationships.
> - To consider four strategies for developing a supporting educational environment.

WHY THIS CHAPTER?

Presumably you are reading this book based on your interest in LGBTQI+-inclusive Relationship and Sex Education. We may not, so far, be taking quite the form you imagined, in that we started the book looking at self, before considering gender, both in a very general sense. And now we aren't even going to get straight to the nitty-gritty sex bit. We will get there, do not fear. However, first we must consider the mountainous mass of fallacy that is perpetuated around **romantic** relationships and associated perceptions of sexual norms. What we are desperately trying to escape, in this book, is all the nonsense that has been built up (yes, that biopsychosocial rubbish) that we all believe about what everybody else is doing, or not doing, in their private and romantic lives. Our hope is that we enable you to break down and free from those façades and untruths that we are teaching our children and young people of today. Again, we ask you to reflect on exactly where we are currently getting our sex and relationship education from (all of us, not just children and young people). Think about media, reality TV shows, commercialism (sex sells), pornography, modern music videos, movies, and so on, before we take a look at reality.

In this chapter we are going to focus on romantic relationships. We use the term 'relationship' to describe any type of connection between two or more people, which includes everything from a one-off meeting/connection to a marriage of several decades. We use the term 'romantic' here to suggest the nature of the relationship, that there is some interpersonal attraction which draws the people in relationship to connect – this might include everything from a fleeting physical sexual desire to deep love and spiritual magnetism. We are being mindfully cautious in our definitions, so they may read a little clunkily as unfortunately we do not have a suitable term in the English language to describe just what we are aiming for, which is something that encompasses intimacy, romance and everything in between. However, what we wish to explore, in this Lesson in Love & Understanding, are all the various ways in which human beings have (what we will term) 'romantic relationships' and the different expressions of love within these. Only by looking at things from a relational perspective, first, can we be truly inclusive of everybody. The risk of focusing directly on sex (**sexual intercourse**) is that we fail to recognise all the millions of people who are not having any kind of sex, either inside or outside of romantic relationships for a variety of reasons, and the minute we do that we are falling straight back into the snare and perpetuating this crazy loop of miseducation. Romantic relationships are not all about sex. Let's erase this kind of Freudian assumption from our minds. This is not an easy chapter to read, as we invite you to rethink everything society has conditioned you to believe as true about sex; and to be aware of all the subliminal messaging we live among that suggests we should conform to the alleged sexual norms belonging to our respective categories of age, gender, sexuality, relationship status, faith group, and so on.

IS THERE ANYTHING NORMAL ABOUT 'NORMS'?

Much of this is about our idea of 'norms'. We have studied the facts and figures about the different types of relationships recorded in the UK. The data from the Office for National Statistics (2019) provides an interesting insight into the sexuality of the UK population, providing a range of information about geographical location, age, density and so forth. However, such statistics are only superficial and are unlikely to be statistically significant if more robust data analysis was conducted – for example, when were you last asked about your relationship, gender, sexuality or sex demographics? Furthermore, with statistics, there is no explanation as to the 'why' in their interpretation.

Consequently, we feel the statistics are not within our interest for RSE – they are extraneous to our discussion; we thought it helpful to explain why.

What we should be doing from the very beginning of any kind of formal education is exploring what love is, and what it means, as well as what it is not, and recognising unloving behaviour. The focus is equally on loving oneself as it is on treating others with love and respect, and expecting that respect in return. As Eleanor Roosevelt once said: 'The giving of love is an education in itself.' These lessons are fundamental to our very being, crucial for healthy development, and all children, all people deserve Lessons in Love & Understanding. Now you may be saying to yourself, 'Well, I'm already doing that with my child/class.' And yes, we do not doubt that you are. However, are you confident that you are educating from the whole scope of romantic relational possibility, including families that do not look like your own family system? We all have blind spots in our own prejudice and thought patterns; indeed, you may be familiar with the **Johari window**. There are times our political slant might give different meaning to the information we deliver. And many times we omit crucial pieces of information that are unconsciously or consciously not so accessible to us for a personal reason. We are only human, after all (although teachers are pretty special humans!). However, in making the choice to not educate children in what other people believe, and how other people live and relate to one another, we are not fully educating our students about the world.

OUR RESPONSIBILITY TO THE NEW GENERATION

As parents and educators, we also have the desire to adequately guide our young people in the way that we find most important, safe for them spiritually, mentally and physically, and in keeping with our own ethics and morals. So, what qualifies us to do this? Many would argue that their spiritual and religious learning and understanding allow for them to be best placed to provide relationship, sexuality and gender education. Until now, though, there was no such guidance across faith and culture. As parents and home educators, there are limits to what one can provide, as we have identified previously. We each have our own set of learning experiences, and therefore understanding and perception of the world. This is a beautiful thing and, as educators, it's our job to allow our pupils and students to recognise their own version of life, and to celebrate the ways in which they find similarities and differences in their thoughts, feelings and views, as compared with others. Please see Lessons in Love & Understanding 1 for more on this theme.

In the UK, there is an ongoing debate about what is appropriate to teach at the Key Stage 1 and Key Stage 2 levels, in terms of Relationship and Sex Education (RSE). Some sections of faith groups continue to protest because UK law states that RSE should contain LGBT representation in the view of equality. Opinions opposing this law and learning are that it is discriminating against the religious beliefs of certain groups to do so, as they believe identifying as LGBTQI+ is immoral in view of the religious teachings that they wish their children to adhere to. Many schools, teachers and educators in the UK have been feeling under immense pressure over this ethical dilemma and have been forced into difficult positions in order to protect their pupils from the repercussions of group protests outside school buildings. The BBC television programme *Panorama*, 15 July 2019, asked 'What is the answer?' We've got an answer right here in this chapter, so do read on.

CULTURAL VALUES

What we are currently experiencing in Western culture by the neglect of this part of the curriculum is the growing problem that today's youth have the back-to-front, upside-down and topsy-turvy experience of ESR rather than RSE. That is, with both formal and social education lacking, young people are going online to learn, finding (within very easy reach) internet pornography, which is completely unreflective of 'normal', healthy, consensual sex, and in turn potentially damaging learning about loving, and relationships with both the self and others. All of today's children and young people in the Western world risk exposure to this, regardless of what measures parents and teachers take to prevent access to pornographic materials. Internet access = potential exposure to pornography. The only safeguard against this is education. We have a responsibility, as a society, to protect our children from the dangers of what has crept into modern life as a perversion of perceived relationship norms. By norm, what we mean is the facts on what healthy relationships look and feel like in reality – i.e. not the headteacher receiving double penetration from the caretaker and school secretary during lunch hour. If you are unaware of exactly what we are talking about, have a quick internet search (privately, outside of work and school property, of course) and see just how easy it is to access pornography. Two clicks on a Google search takes you to hardcore porn, with no age ID or financial exchange required. The huge risk we run by not teaching children anything about RSE and normal loving relationships (across the full spectrum of different types of relationship) is that hardcore pornography becomes the norm. So, kids know two things about sex: it's not good to talk about it, and it is a purely physical (often disrespectful or aggressive) and loveless act outside of romantic relationships. There are so many reasons that this seems such a sad view of sexual intimacy for anybody to have, regardless of their age, identity, cultural background or religious beliefs.

Most adults are also aware through personal, if not professional, experience, that telling a human being of any age to just not do something, with no explanation or education around why, has never been an effective method of moral guidance since the beginning of time. The force of parents, teachers and friends is nothing against the mighty puberty, either. Thus, the key is to facilitate our children and young people to make educated choices about their future relationships. This is a beautiful thing and, as educators, it's our job to allow our pupils and students to recognise their own version of life, and to celebrate the ways in which they find similarities and differences in their thoughts, feelings and views, as/from others. Please see Lesson 1 for more on this theme. This then builds on looking at identity and the things that make each individual the unique being they are, which might include belonging to other groups, be that faith, gender, interest, culture, and so on. There is then the very important step in considering exactly what one looks for in any type of relationship. This often comes with a personal reflection on one's family of origin and the values one has learnt from the relationships within the family. We invite you to take some time for personal reflection with the following prompts for guidance:

- What qualities were most important to you as a child from your main caregivers in their relationship with you?
- Are there any traits or values that you would consider important for future family or romantic relationships?

- How would you know that you are happy within a romantic relationship?
- What is your attachment style (do you like a lot of independence or desire to be frequently in close proximity to people you love)?
- What kind of boundaries might you require around potential romantic relationships?

The list could continue endlessly, but what we encourage you to consider is your own personal needs, along with your values and desires within a romantic relationship. There are no right or wrong answers – this is entirely personal and it is not set in stone, of course. This may change over time and be influenced by the people we meet and how we develop as human beings in the world. The importance is in reinforcing that we are all different and find attraction to different personalities for different reasons. We have diverse needs within romantic relationships, so it is absolutely valid to decide that a romantic relationship is not something desirable at all. Many people do so, and an even higher percentage of people would consider themselves in an asexual romantic relationship (some co-habiting, others not), whereby there is some form of contract of being in a loving relationship without a sexual element to that union. So, let's not get bogged down with the S in RSE, because we are falling into the porn-trap by doing so. Let's recognise that here in the real world there are many people who find compatibility, live in healthy romantic relationships and find deep interpersonal and spiritual fulfilment in this. That includes people of different genders, people of the same gender, people who live alone or have long distance, short-term, or lifelong relationships, people who have arranged marriages, or unions of mutual convenience, people who live with more than one partner, people who engage in sexual relationships and those who do not. Have we covered everybody? We aim to. All of the above is normal – completely normal – that is fact. That is not to say that this sits comfortably with everybody's personal, political, cultural and spiritual beliefs. However, we hope you are getting the gist that we champion embracing our wonderful range of diversity as human beings in human relationships. Our vision is for every child to feel celebrated for who they truly are, in all their essence, and to feel empowered to make the right choices for them – with a comprehensive education on people in the world around them, enabling us all to live in harmony.

EDUCATION AND RELATIONSHIPS

Formal education has always included geography, history, modern studies, and religious education; later, subjects such as psychology and sociology became offered as part of secondary school education. As a human race, we have always been fascinated in studying language and communications. We send shuttles into outer space looking for other life forms. We learn so much through our curiosity about ways of living that are different from our own – just think of the popularity of sci-fi, cosplay and virtual realities. These are recognised ways of delving into the fantasy of otherness. We all know of some keen Trekkies, Star Wars enthusiasts and Harry Potter fans. Sci-fi and fantasy are accepted and celebrated forms of popular literature – and as educators we have shown that offering a wide range of genres allows students to expand their creative and imaginative minds, growing their capacity for learning. One does not become what they read (although it's rather fun to imagine a classroom of wizards, cats in hats and Gruffalos, all being taught by the Hobbit). We use literature and the arts to create our own unique meaning in life. As human beings, healthy education allows us to see that we are exactly like no other, and that we will never fully understand what it is like to live the life of another, although we also recognise the wisdom in acquiring knowledge, understanding and compassion for our fellow beings. Raeni's voice gives strength to this sentiment:

> At my new school I was the only black kid, the only Rasta, and the only kid whose mother served their father, Queen to King. Our livity was strange to my peers. My family welcomed my new friends to our home. We ate some food and listened to some reggae music. We all had a nice time, but I felt sad because they judged the ways of my family, our culture . . . especially my parents and the respect we show to my Dada. My Madda would say 'Feel no way, Raeni', but I did not like anyone to think bad of my family and think my Dada do us wrong . . . just because we were different. (Raeni, age 22)

It is so important that, throughout our lives, we are educated about the people around us and that we are taught about one another's cultures and beliefs and the changes in our world over time, within our local communities as well as outwardly to the global community. It is of utmost importance that our future generations learn of the real world they live in, and that they have an understanding of themselves and one another, in order that we can live safely and peacefully side by side, and make positive connections as we work together on this shared journey of life. This is one of the tips for RSE for all: let's empower children and young people to share their feelings, to discuss, to debate, to find resolutions where they find conflict and difference with others. Let's teach our children to think.

REPRESENTATION AND INCLUSION OF ALL GROUPS

In considering social education on relationships, families and community, it is vital to fairly represent all groups within society. To deliberately omit representation of any person, family or group because of their race, religion, culture, gender, sexuality, disability, or indeed any feature that might deem them as a minority or specialist group is, at best, ignorant discrimination and, at worst, bullying and abusive. It is not acceptable to say that it is in breach of one's faith or belief system to acknowledge the existence and identity of others. It is also extremely bad modelling for children to witness adults express hostility towards schools, educators and teachers, for providing fair and impartial RSE for pupils belonging to a diverse range of backgrounds.

> As a dedicated geography teacher, in a committed polyamorous relationship, it is often one of my partners that attends school events to support our own primary school aged children, as I am at work in my own classroom at the high school where I work. Other parents don't question any of this – I guess they are used to step-parents and other carers, I don't know, I've never asked them. Our close friends know and support our family. I've never seen the need to talk to my colleagues about my private life. The notion that anybody would think I was sub-standard as a parent, or that there was anything weird, perverted or damaging about our kids being brought up by 4 loving adults, in a harmonious house, is small minded and ignorant. I feel primary schools ought to teach RSE in a way which is love focused and inclusive of all families. (Alex, age 58)

The fears or perceived risks of educating children on the norms of relationships seem largely to relate to discussion of **sexual activity**.

Let's take a moment to ask ourselves about this. What kind of assumptions do we make about families that show differences or similarities to our own? Our society is still holding on to the pretence of a heteronormative, two-children norm. For example, according to the Office for National Statistics (2019), the 'typical' family (of which there are 19.1 million) has 1.9 children with women having their first child at 28.8 years old. According to YouGov (2019), the family are most likely to drive a VW Golf or Ford Fiesta; prefer films by Steven Spielberg; like books by Roald Dahl; enjoy television programmes by David Attenborough; prefer listening to Adele, Coldplay, Abba or Queen, depending on their mood; enjoy eating Maltesers; get their shopping from Aldi; brush their teeth using Colgate; read either the *Metro* or *The Guardian*; like shopping at Marks & Spencer; opt for Samsung gadgets; specifically use Google Maps as their main app; and stay at a Premier Inn rather than any other hotel. If we are talking about you – sorry, but you're Mrs, Mr, Mx Average. If you know someone like this, wow. Of course, such norms are problematic as a person may be a norm on one scale but completely way off at the fringe on another. If we take, for example, a family that represents this perceived norm, in the public eye, what is it that we assume about this family that make them a more appropriate example of being a family than, say, a same-sex couple with a 'blended' family who might even shop at Tesco and drive an Audi? It can be useful to write a list of the assumptions we might have, and the ideas attached to our outsider's glance at any family unit. A large part of that is our assumptions about sexuality and gender and expressions of those. To re-emphasise, we are not going to discuss sexuality within this chapter and will do so within Chapter 4.

The most important elements to consider in relation to education are:

- What love is and what it is not (safeguarding against abusive behaviours and domestic violence).
- Different types of love and how people communicate this in life (friendships, committing to be a family, ceremonies, etc.).
- Self-love and creating boundaries around relational needs.
- Exploring feelings, emotions and when love hurts.
- Respecting that romantic relationships come in many different shapes and forms.

It is important to be mindful that all of us are walking about carrying a huge relationship and social history, dating back to the earliest story retold, or as played out in the behaviours of our early caregivers. Everything that has gone before influences the choices that we make and the way we perceive interactions with others. It doesn't matter if you are the 4-year-old at kindergarten or the 64-year-old class teacher – none of us enter into any kind of human relationship with a *tabula rasa*. It can be helpful for anybody to look at their current family system and as far back on their family tree as possible. Creating your own genogram allows different relationships, patterns and psychological links to be pictorially represented, and this can provide great insight into the internalised beliefs many of us hold, which we have learnt through our family systems. Sometimes these are referred to as 'oughts and nots' – things that we were brought up thinking we ought to do and things that we were taught we definitely should not do. This is not meant be a tool for casting judgements, but rather curious observations that allow insight and understanding relating to one's own beliefs and how those might be played out in relationships or appear through 'leakage' when we are teaching. Leakage (a counselling term) is when we inadvertently share information that is biased by our own personal belief systems or opinions. As teachers and educators we have a responsibility to become aware of the ways in which we may do this, so we can guard against influencing our students based on our own personal and biased ideologies, and create a platform of possibility in which the student can find their own truths. All genograms are enlightening as they have the possibility to represent a far deeper level of truth than a traditional family tree. This is safest explored in a therapeutic setting for privacy purposes (therefore, not an exercise for your next staff team meeting). However, we will provide some creative and safe ways of exploring family systems for the classroom.

Here are some general considerations to make all of this come alive in your educational environment, followed by some lesson plans, inclusive of all:

1. Involve the parents and guardians of your pupils/students by sending home guidance about how they can support their child's relationship education with some fun home exercises to enjoy within the family unit. It is important that these learning activities do not need to be fed back to the teacher, as that would suggest

there are right or wrong answers, or a desired way to go about the learning activity. This is about personalising the exercises to fit the families' unique way of doing things within their system, and they should take ownership of this learning as a family unit.

2. Often, for teachers and educators, we are only involved in family matters when there is an issue to resolve. For example, a problem at school or at home that requires communication between educator and family, or a safeguarding issue that is raised. It can leave us with a negative outlook of family life in general, because we are rarely involved when all is going swimmingly. It's great to shift that focus and encourage pupils/students to pull out the positive values and things that stand out as important to them in relational values. All of the interactions we have with our families of origin/main caregivers inform the way we behave in future relationships. Consideration of how one likes to be treated and affirmation of how it feels to be loved boosts self-esteem, enabling young people to make the best choices for their well-being.

3. Explore all different types of family structures and ensure that different types of families are represented in the media and literature you are using in your educational setting. Emphasise the fact that the quality of love and care received from a caregiver/parent/guardian towards a child does not relate to that person's age, race, culture, gender, relationship status, sexuality, disability, etc. All of us live in unique and ever-changing family systems, and there are an infinite number of ways of being normal. Phew!

4. In Chapter 6 we advise you how to incorporate a greater degree of equality and diversity into your school policy and how to gain support, getting families on-side in the promotion of an inclusive school and wider community.

CONCLUSION

This chapter has specifically focused on what is meant by romantic relationships and the various and diverse forms these take. We discussed how, as teachers, we can facilitate the exploration of 'love', what it means and what it does not. Indeed, we have a professional duty as educators which is fundamentally more important than any academic subject – that is, to enable students to recognise and appreciate their version of the world, and to be aware of their thoughts, perceptions, feelings and perspectives. This includes appreciating similarities and differences in others, which harmonise and enable a greater perspective and appreciation of life and different ways of living and being.

Delivering education that supports young people in developing meaningful relationships requires helping pupils to explore their personal belief systems, boundaries and relational needs. As educators, we can all benefit from examining our own romantic relationships, patterns, beliefs, blind spots and prejudices. With a deepened level of personal awareness, we can ensure that we teach from a place of fair and loving kindness.

KEY POINTS

- We have a responsibility to foster the new generation in developing healthy relationships.
- Education is critical in helping students explore and understand relationships.
- All groups should be included and represented when considering relationships.
- As teachers, there are simple ways to support relationship education: involve parents/guardians, ensure that there are positive interactions with students' families, explore different types of family structure irrespective of a range of social and cultural factors, continue to promote an inclusive school.

LESSONS IN LOVE & UNDERSTANDING 3: RELATIONSHIPS

(For the RSE teaching that we advocate, 4-year-olds can be included in the KS1 learning, and 17-year-olds can be included in the KS4 learning.)

KS1 (AGE 5–7 YEARS)

- Provide a large paper love heart and ask pupils to fill it up with pictures, drawings, words, and colours that represent things that they love. Provide guidance that this might be people, animals, places, activities, colours or feelings – absolutely anything that they love. Once complete, discuss the unique nature of each love heart and the things that are important to different people. Discuss different degrees of love and how love for chocolate cake might be different from love for a parent or family member.

- Hold a mindfulness meditation or guided visualisation exercise in which pupils are invited to find a place of love and explore the senses that may be associated with this. Discuss the meditation and invite pupils to channel that positive feeling of love towards their peers and to think about the effect of words on how somebody might feel, in a good or bad way (available online at: www.lessonsinlove.info)

- Love rules: ask the class to work on creating rules that will help everybody know that they are loved. First, think about behaviours and things one might say that do not show love and then come up with alternative loving ways. Introduce the concept of respect and explore what this means.

- Ensure that literature and all teaching materials are delivered in a way that represents all types of relationships and family units (see Additional reading).

KS2 (AGE 7–11 YEARS)

- Discuss the terms 'love' and 'respect' – work with different definitions, perhaps asking the class to research or discuss in pairs. Within your class or a group of pupils who know one another, provide a piece of A4 paper and ask each pupil to put their full name on the top. Everybody should then pass the sheet of paper one place to their left. Ask the student to look at the name on their paper and, with love and respect, write down one quality about the named student which they appreciate or admire. Once complete, the papers are passed to the left again and the process is repeated until everybody has their own named piece of paper back. Allow time for the pupils to silently read the comments written about them. Then facilitate a group discussion about how it feels to read loving and respectful things about themselves. How might it feel to read hateful, disrespectful things? How does this effect how we feel and how we might behave as a result?

(Continued)

- Ask pupils to draw the people and animals that they live with, labelling who they are. Highlight to the group that all family units look different and that it is common to live with neither birth parents, one birth parent, or two or more birth parents, as well as step-parents, other family members or friends. Families come in many shapes and forms. Invite pupils to write a creative piece about what makes their family unit special and unique.

- Teach an online safety session helping young people to be aware of who they are engaging with online. Highlight the very positive aspects of social networking and that many people do form healthy and fulfilling relationships of all kinds online. Provide young people with various online sources for help and support if they sense they are in any kind of danger or are being bullied online or elsewhere. From an online perspective, most UK schools teach the SMART rules: Safe, Meeting, Accepting, Reliable, Tell. For more guidance, visit www.kidsmart.org.uk

- Ensure that literature and all teaching materials are delivered in a way that represents all types of relationships and family units. Several books are available that may help, such as *The Great Big Book of Families* by Mary Hoffman and Ros Asquith, *Love Makes a Family* by Sophie Beer, *The Family Book* by Todd Parr, *And Tango Makes Three* by Justin Richardson and other similar books.

- Help pupils to become familiar with terms to describe different relationships, such as platonic, monogamous, polyamorous, or long-distance.

KS3 (AGE 11–14 YEARS)

- Run some research groups, looking for different definitions of love, using as many different types of sources as possible, including religious texts and a variety of different genres. Collect different statements about love from famous people past and present, and ask groups to define love as best they can. Ask whether there are different types of love. Is love different in different cultures/countries? Is there a difference between love and attraction? (Emphasise that we are not talking about sex until the next session; here, we are talking about relationships.)

- Use the prompts on the cards provided and ask a group to role play an improvisation based on the given characters and scenarios. Once the scene is played out, ask the students to identify loving behaviour and unloving behaviour. Discuss boundaries and acceptable ways to behave, and see whether the group can find a resolution to any issues raised.

- Ask the class to research the different types of relationship union ceremonies they can find, perhaps in groups, looking at the beliefs associated with different types of ceremony and the meaning of the ceremony. Then set the class to debate whether the legal age for marriage should be raised to 25. Here we examine our ideas around age, life experience and relationship commitments.
- Write, draw or perform a creative piece about love, equality and diversity

KS4 (AGE 14–16 YEARS)

- Task the class to think about a romantic relationship that they know of from either real life or fiction (a book, film, or TV show, for example). Ask the class to write about the values that they respect about the relationship they have chosen, and what advice they might give the people in the relationship for a successful future together.
- Teach a lesson on coping when relationships dissolve. Think about the wider impact on family systems or friendship groups when this happens, and problem solve as a group, creating a list of tips in tackling the challenges that you identify might come up for people involved in a relationship ending.
- Talk about the difference between loving behaviours and abusive behaviours. Educate on domestic violence and where young people can go for support and how they can support one another (see the Additional reading in Chapter 8).

With this age group, often an individual or the class have ideas about themes or topics they would like to cover. It is fantastic if you can go with this and let the students take the lead on their RSE and lesson plan.

ADDITIONAL READING
KS1 (AGE 5–7 YEARS)

- *Mommy, Mama, and Me* by Leslea Newman.
- *Daddy, Papa, and Me* by Leslea Newman.
- *Families, Families, Families* by Suzanne Lang.

- *Queen of the Hanukkah Dosas* by Pamela Ehrenberg.
- *Love Makes a Family* by Sophie Beer.

KS2 (AGE 7–11 YEARS)

- *Drama* by Raina Telgemeier.
- *We Are Family* by Patricia Hegarty.
- *Lizard Radio* by Pat Schmatz.
- *Zenobia July* by Lisa Bunker.
- *George* by Alex Gino.
- *Gracefully Grayson* by Ami Polonsky.

KS3/4 (AGE 11–16 YEARS)

- *Proud* by Juno Dawson.
- *Parrotfish* by Ellen Wittlinger
- *Freakboy* by Kristin Elizabeth Clark.
- *Luna* by Julie Anne Peters.
- *Almost Perfect* by Brian Katcher.
- *Queer: The Ultimate LGBT Guide for Teens* by Kathy Belge, Marke Bieschke and Christisan Robinson.
- *Sticks and Stones . . . and Words That Hurt Me: A Collection of Poetry and Short Stories in Support of Domestic Violence Awareness* by Aurelia Maria Casey.
- *Colour Outside The Lines: Stories about Love* by Sangu Mandanna.
- *Alex As Well* by Alyssa Brugman.
- *Happy Families* by Tanita S. Davis.

ADULTS

- *The Whole-Brain Child: 12 Proven Strategies to Nuture Your Child's Developing Mind* by Daniel Siegel and Tina Payne Bryson.
- *The Power and Purpose of the Teenage Brain* by Daniel Siegel. Available online at: www.youtube.com/watch?v=_r_FmiJkD6s (date accessed: 28 October 2019).
- *The Developing Mind: How Relationships and the Brain Interact to Shape Who We Are (2nd edn)* by Daniel Siegel.
- *How to Avoid Falling in Love with a Jerk (2nd revised edn)* by John Van Epp.

4

SEXUALITY AND SEX

CONTENTS

- Why this chapter?
- A return to identity
- Sexuality
- An explanation of sexuality and the need not to explain one's sexuality
- The campaigning paradox
- Key Stage 1 Sex Education (age 5–7 years)
- Key Stage 2 Sex Education (age 7–11 years)
- Key Stage 3 Sex Education (age 11–14 years)
- Key Stage 4 Sex Education (age 14–16 years)
- Conclusion

CHAPTER OBJECTIVES

- To understand the counterparts of sexuality: social identity, behaviour/practice and fantasy/desire.
- To appreciate that sexuality does not need a justification: it is what it is.
- To understand the campaigning paradox for equal rights.
- To consider the role of appropriate sex education across the Key Stages.
- To examine effective practises of effective sex education.

WHY THIS CHAPTER?

If you have been reading from the start, and not skipped straight to this chapter, you may be thinking 'Finally, we got there'. There is great deliberation in our structure and approach, because we need to be rainbow clear that this is not a book about delivering LGBT sex education. This is a book about teaching real RSE: how human beings relate and react to one another and about the different ways that people, love, companionship and family systems thrive. Sexual attraction and behaviour is a part of that, but far from the full picture, as we hope to have demonstrated in Chapters 1–3. In Chapter 4 we consider sexual attraction and defining sexuality, before looking at appropriate and meaningful sex education for our students of the 2020s.

A RETURN TO IDENTITY

As discussed in Chapter 2, the acronym LGBTQI+ can feel pretty confusing, as it describes so many things. We have Lesbian, Gay, Bisexual – OK, relational and categories of sexuality. Then we have Transgender. Hmm, so we have gender in there, which is nothing to do with sexuality. And Queer – another wide category, followed by Intersex, which is then including a medical element; then we have a mysterious plus sign, referring to what exactly? It's not to say that anybody who identifies in any one or more of those cohorts would necessary feel any belonging to the collaborative terminology.

However, the political and sociological effect of the clubbing together of those experiencing discrimination, isolation and hate targeted through gender, sexuality and sex has been of vital importance and significance, as outlined in Chapter 5, and as described in Chapter 2 when we consider gender labels.

SEXUALITY

When one is asked the question of one's sexuality by a stranger or on a generic form it can feel rather personal and, frankly, unnecessary. After all, it's surely only courteous to at least ask a person out for a drink before enquiring about their sexual preferences. The language of sexology and the definitions can be unhelpful. The word 'sex', alone, is troublesome. Many of the terms describing sexuality refer to relational attraction that may or may not involve sexual practice. They are also not clear-cut binary terms. Very often, the way in which somebody may sexually identify is not reflective of sexual practice or a full picture of sexual desire. We find it helpful to consider sexuality in three components: social identity, behaviour/practice and fantasy/desire (see Figure 4.1).

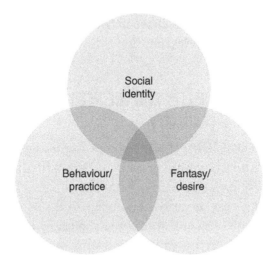

Figure 4.1   Three counterparts of sexuality

So, for example, a man who identifies as **heterosexual** and has only ever had female sexual partners and romantic relationships may concurrently have sexual fantasies about other men and people identifying as genders other than female. Or somebody identifying as asexual and aromantic may also regularly masturbate and have sexual and relational fantasies that they have no intention of acting on. When you look at the overlap between the circles in the Venn diagram in Figure 4.1, you can see that there are many possibilities within this, and each individual might be able to think about if there are concurrencies and differences when considering their own unique sexuality using this model. Furthermore, although the circles are of equal size, any one circle could be larger or smaller than the others depending on the relevance of that component at any specific time.

We chose this as our preferred model quite simply as it makes a lot of sense, despite the delusion of heteronormativity we are tricked by. And, as with all constituents of our personal identity, these are not fixed labels and traits. It is possible for identity, practice and desire to change or develop. This is not to say that sexuality is something cognitive or a 'life choice'. As human beings, we do not have the power or ability to fully understand the phenomenon of human attraction and love. 'Great,' we hear you say – 'so how am I meant to teach that?' We can only suggest, with an open heart and an open mind. It is unnecessary to find out exactly why such variance in gender and sexuality exists in your role as educator. The fact that we know it does, and human beings of past, present and future always have and always will identify in a whole spectrum of ways, is all we need to know in order to warrant educational inclusion in understanding this aspect of humanity.

AN EXPLANATION OF SEXUALITY AND THE NEED NOT TO EXPLAIN ONE'S SEXUALITY

In Chapter 5 you will learn the history of pathology and the many past attempts at understanding gender and sexuality through biology and psychiatry. We have moved on from those days and understand that human beings are mystifyingly, beautifully complex; and the ways in which we relate to one another, on so many different levels, is fascinating and only to be understood through observation (disclaimer – this is not meant in a literal sense, we are not endorsing voyeurism). To go back to the intrusive questionnaire/ID forms asking about gender and sexuality, much of this type of collection of demographics is for the purpose of gaining data that allows us to statistically demonstrate or evidence representation of LGBTQI+ communities, to give us a better idea of the bigger picture of reality, and in order to reflect what real relationships look like in their various forms within society. So, what we are saying is that it is not your job to explain why anybody has the sexuality or gender identity that they do, or why they may or may not represent this in their everyday living. If we stick with the facts and represent families of all different formations, we allow young people to embrace all sections of society. We also allow learners to understand themselves and those around them better, on an interpersonal and relational level. This is no different from teaching religious education. It is important for all human beings to understand and respect those of all faiths or no faith at all. Religious education has never been a method of evangelising or converting children, nor do teachers need to have all the answers about spirituality and scripture. It is equally important that we don't make assumptions about individual people and their belief systems because of how they might religiously identify. For example, somebody might identify as being Jewish, yet still like to join in Christmas festivities with their neighbours, as the celebration does not make them feel uncomfortable, threaten their identity or spoil their enjoyment of partying. This does not make them a Christian – they are still Jewish and they may invite the neighbours to Hanukkah celebrations in return. This is showing love, and we should respect the views and identities of others, and not make assumptions based on their way of identifying – be that culture, faith, class, gender, sexuality, and so on.

THE CAMPAIGNING PARADOX

It often feels as though LGBTQI+ is a double-edged sword. The campaign for equal rights, inclusion and a just law means that completely ordinary people have had to make themselves stand out as being somehow abnormal in order to raise awareness and visibility of LGBTQI+ communities. Supporters of those communities that identify as cis-heterosexual are known as allies, which can give the sad implication that the rest of the cis-heterosexual community are enemies. We are only too aware of the threat of such hostility. It seems shocking, and disappointing, that in the year 2020, as professional academics working as subject matter experts in education, health and well-being, a factual book of this nature could be deemed as controversial in any way. And so with that, let's move on to the focus of the taboo: sex education.

Many of you are covering lots already and using RSE packages that your school has devised or bought in. However, with the introduction of RSE 2020, it's likely that the content will need to be reviewed and revised, using content from this book. We will offer guidance in what we would recommend to be included, in addition to what you are already doing, making no assumptions about what you currently cover – fantastic if you are already doing this.

KEY STAGE 1 SEX EDUCATION (AGE 5–7 YEARS)

Currently, at Key Stage 1, children are often educated about babies and their development from nought to five years. This kind of teaching often runs alongside activities such as planting seeds and watching them grow, and generally thinking about living growth and development. Key Stage 1 education has a lot of information about emotional growth and understanding one's feelings, and there also tends to be plenty of information around boundaries and safety – e.g. keeping one's privates private, asking and giving permission to be embraced/massaged. Key Stage 1 lessons on appropriate behaviours are important features, too. All of this is super, and you teachers and educators know the level at which to pitch to individual pupils, according to their learning and developmental stages and needs. What we are going to do in this chapter is add some extra information in order to make your RSE as inclusive and appropriate as possible.

From as young as nursery or kindergarten some children will have been told by their parents or carers exactly how they were created, including the method of conception. Other children will never be told such information within their family system. And many learn different versions at varying points between those dichotomies, formally and informally. Families tend to have their own belief systems and traditions around what is appropriate to share with a child and at what age. In Western culture, the classic examples are the Tooth Fairy and Father Christmas. There exists a belief that allowing this magic and fantasy is a part of childhood innocence to be enjoyed, alongside conflicting opinion that this is telling children untruths and buying into commercialism. Parents and guardians are very protective of their children's innocence. Introducing anything that does not sit comfortably with the family values and belief systems can be perceived as an infringement on the rights of that family/child. So, if one's feeling is that Key Stage 1 is an age for innocence and to live in fairytale fantasy, it is completely understandable that the concept of introducing anything relating to sexual intercourse is utterly horrifying. That depends, of course, on the parent/educator's own associations with sexual intercourse and perceived fears around this (as discussed in Chapter 3). Sadly, some children will have already experienced sexual abuse and/or witnessed pornographic materials through accident or neglect – and this is a separate issue that we address in Chapters 5 and 6. However, the safety element of teaching children their rights to their body and privacy and boundaries around this is a vital lesson for all Key Stage 1 pupils – as is teaching massage and meditation that is multi-faith, accessible to all levels of ability, and promotes positive association around body, mind and soul – at the same time reinforcing personal boundaries and enabling children to say if they do not wish to touch, be touched or to participate.

In the innocence of Key Stage 1, there will be some children who have accidentally discovered (as we all know, children that age tend to stick their fingers everywhere and anywhere) the pleasurable experience of **masturbation**. Some of you will be nodding, perhaps cringing, as you had that awkward moment in class and had to call in a parent under your safeguarding policy. Or perhaps you were the parent and did not know quite how to deal with this, as the child was only doing what is instinctual and natural, without any of the associations or understanding an older child might have. We have two strategies for teaching in this area. Option one is to incorporate into the privacy and appropriate behaviour lesson that touching or rubbing one's own private zones in front of other people is only appropriate in certain situations – for example, with a towel when getting dried after a swim in a public/communal area. The other method is using a picture system, working one-to-one with pupils. This is particularly helpful for some children with ASD or a preference for visual information. You can make these cards yourself, drawing a series of pictures showing that in the bathroom or private area is where someone would masturbate, and not in the middle of the classroom or the supermarket. If these rules can be understood preceding an incident, it can prevent children later feeling ashamed, and also give a positive message about normal bodily sensations without demonising the behaviour and so preserve innocence.

In a similar effort to keep our children innocent, safe and well, it is crucial that we represent all types of family systems in their everyday schooling. As we have discussed at length in Chapter 3, there is absolutely no need to talk about sexual acts when discussing any family unit, so why would it cause any harm for a child to be aware of families that look different in structure from their own? LGBTQI+ families are massively underrepresented in popular media and especially in schools. How must that feel if, for example, you have two mums and a dad or a single-parent trans male dad, and you constantly have to explain to people who your 'real mum' is or why you 'don't have a mum'? It should not be up to a Key Stage 1 pupil, or any individual, to educate the school and surrounding community on the fact that their family is as valid as any other. This is the current situation that many LGBTQI+ families, as well as some cis single-parents, co-parents, blended-families, step-families, foster and adoption families face, because we are completely failing children in not reflecting the true society in the media and education they receive. May we say it a little louder: there is absolutely no need to talk about sex or how children were (or were not) conceived when we discuss different types of family units. It's neither appropriate nor relevant. Some families have children, some do not. Children come to belong in families in a variety of different ways. Owning one's gender or sexual identity is not like selling a sex tape or world-exclusive tabloid fertility story, but while we continue to conceal real family system norms like some dirty secret, that's the conclusion that society will come to with a lack of education. And that is grossly unfair.

KEY STAGE 2 SEX EDUCATION (AGE 7–11 YEARS)

Key Stage 2 is a prominent period in adolescence, being a normal age for puberty onset. Diverse Sex Development (DSD) might be picked up when patterns do not appear to be normal towards later teenage years (see Chapter 2 for further information) starting from as early as 8 or 9 years old. Most children hit several social milestones while preparing to move to high school and towards the teenage years. It is a time of endings, leaving infanthood and those early developmental stages behind for a far more sophisticated grasp on learning and level of social awareness. Schoolteachers have to be perceptive and astute in gauging where each individual child is on this journey. Maturity differs so greatly from child to child, and developmental rates take different paces and courses, with hormonal bursts and unrecognisable moods and emotions thrown into the mix. It is a time of the unknown and a crucial time for some educational intervention before breasts, periods, bass-tone voices and erections make their clumsy appearance, along with the delights of spotty skin, sweaty 'pits and an unexpected bloom of body fur. Nature can indeed be cruel. Currently, RSE provision differs from school to school with no geographical or standardised expectation of exactly what is taught or when. It would appear that most schools offer Key Stage 2 education on puberty at around 10/11 years of age, with boys and girls separated into groups to hear about how they can expect their bodies to develop and some lessons on personal hygiene accordingly. Some UK schools and many American and European schools offer Sex Education, which includes reproduction and safe sex for heterosexual couples at this same stage – all to differing levels and types of information/style of delivery. So, again we will make no assumptions about what or how much you, the reader, are currently providing as an educator, but will outline what we would professionally consider to be an appropriate level of input at Key Stage 2.

- Talking about sex: what is sex?
- Learning about sex and relationships: respect and boundaries.
- Bodies and sex: puberty and biology.
- Good communication skills and planning to keep safe.
- Sexual activity and safety choices for body and mind.

Beware of that pesky porn trap again and take our top tip: make no assumptions. For those pupils who have no interest in engaging in any sexual act (and this may be temporary or longer term or forever), for whatever reason that may be, there is a risk of sex education lessons sounding like a creepy to-do list. Many children, young people and adults, feel deeply uncomfortable about sexual acts being discussed, and that is acceptable. It's important to express that any reaction to anything that is being delivered is normal. It is also important to give pupils a get out (if they are feeling overwhelmed) and offer an alternative activity, which means that pupils can all receive the information being delivered, but don't need to fully engage as they are doing something related, such as an anatomical word search, for example. We offer further advice for safe space set-up in Chapter 7.

Any children starting to query or already identifying as LGBTQI+ are likely to be feeling self-conscious at best, and dysphoric/hideously distressed at worst. Many young people may be experiencing some degree of minority stress, if sex education is delivered from a hetero-normative lens. A conscious effort must be made to represent normal, healthy and diverse sexual encounters. This is also where our Glossary comes in handy. So many terms that are casually used are unhelpful in the message they give – for example, 'gay sex' being used to describe male-to-male, penile–anal penetration. For a start, males identifying as gay are not restricted to this one sexual manoeuvre – it might get a bit samey after a while. And anal sex – or 'blow job' with no blowing involved – does not belong exclusively to gay men and never has done – confusing! Again, there are often assumptions that this is a female-to-male act. It's not actually gender-specific, as we discussed in Chapter 2. It is possible for somebody identifying as any gender to have a penis and for somebody of any gender to entertain it/its owner. When we don't try to set a repertoire of sexual behaviours on people according to their gender, sexuality and age, it's a lot simpler to understand sex, and to relax about the need to know the unwritten rules or falling into the porn-trap.

The Family Planning Association (FPA) provided the following statistics in 2011 about when school-aged students first engaged in sexual activity:

- The average age of first heterosexual intercourse was 16 for both men and woman.
- Almost a third of men and a quarter of women aged 16–19 years had sexual intercourse before they were 16 years of age.
- Around 80% of young people reported to have used a condom for their first sexual intercourse.
- Almost half of women and one in five men (aged 16–24 years) reported that they wished they had waited longer before first having sex.

So, as we can see, some school-age students are having sex – fact. Yes, it is illegal, even between two consenting students under the age of 16. Yes, we do have a duty of care as teachers if we are aware of such interactions. Yes, we do need to report any concerns, no matter how slight, to the Designated Safeguarding Lead. Let's not panic. However, it might be that your school decides that Key Stage 2 is the right time to deliver sex education, taking these statistics into account.

What good sex education will endorse is:

- Getting to know one's own body, mind and soul, before rushing into anything with anybody else's. There is no hurry and there's normally better reasons to wait until the right time than to do something that is later regretted. It's good to look and learn about normal bodies at this stage (and results in less giggling than starting this at Key Stages 3/4).
- Building a strong sense of personal values and respecting the values of others. Sometimes this is designed as 'rights and responsibilities', so a statement such as 'I have the right to safety within my relationships' can also be read as 'I have the responsibility to keep my partner(s) safe'. This is a broad example, but it is about looking at the things that are important to different people and how we communicate our needs in a fair way.
- Dispelling the myths and examining the influences on modern society and the ideas we might have about relationships, gender and sexuality in relation to sex.
- Examining everything with the awareness of equality and diversity. Ask yourself whether is it appropriate to split groups into girls and boys. If it is, what assumptions are we making about gender and sexuality?

Let's consider the voice of Tara. What needs to change in how we educate in order that otherwise educated 12-year-olds are not engaging in risky sexual behaviours?

I have known I was a bisexual cis-female from a young age, certainly junior school. I first instigated sex with a boy from school when I was 12. I thought I knew it all. I had no proper sex ed at school (a biology lesson, told not to have sex until married – by parents and church) but the attention that came with puberty was too exciting to resist acting on. I felt powerful. The idea that I could have been led astray by boys my age is laughable, as I was actively pursuing sexual experience at any opportunity . . . it 100% was not the boys taking the lead, my other girl friends were way more experimental than the boys we knew. I know my parents and teachers would be shocked to know what was going on. I really believe if adults had been more honest about sex, I wouldn't have got the same buzz out of doing what I did back then and been less curious. A large part of the thrill was doing something I shouldn't be doing . . . without getting caught. When I look back, I know I took a lot of risky chances over my early teens. I also carry a sense of resentment that adults around me were naive enough to let this happen . . . I was 12!!! (Tara, age 22)

There is much that we can change for the better in our RSE provision. In the USA, they believe that Key Stage 2 (or the US equivalent thereof) is a vital time for sound information and education before Key Stage 3 (high school), when it is considered 'too late' in terms of societal norms, pressures and hormonal led curiosity. This seems a wise strategy and is undoubtedly safer than allowing pubescent kids to research the internet with no proper guidance, or finding partners to experiment with, without thinking about or having any awareness of the potential consequences or how that sits with their value system.

KEY STAGE 3 SEX EDUCATION (AGE 11–14 YEARS)

This is when the detail comes and the stuff that most schools are doing already. The emphasis here is on making these lessons current, relevant and engaging for all. With this age group it is possible to work at a far deeper level when considering romantic relationships, and exploring feelings and emotions is essential in keeping these 11–14-year-olds mentally thriving in the chemical chaos their bodies and minds are trying to deal with. It is at this stage that extreme exhaustion is commonly experienced, as the growth and mental processing takes its toll. It can be useful to remember that, as a reader of this book, most of you are likely to have been born at least a couple of decades before the young people you are teaching. The age of onset of puberty is steadily dropping. Research by Herman-Giddens, published by the American Academy of Paediatrics, has found this to be true of boys and girls. In 1860, the average age of girls' puberty onset was 16.6 years. In 1920 it was 14.6, by 1980 it was 12.5 and by 2010 it was 10.5 years (Herman-Giddens et al., 1997). Boys show a similar pattern with around a year behind the girls' average onset (Herman-Giddens et al., 2012). Adolescence lasts far longer, as societal structures have changed with a steady increase in children and young people remaining in the parental family home beyond the age of 16 while in further education, or to aid financial security where housing is not easily available. There are many theories as to why this is, and Daniel Siegel writes in depth about it, and the neurological and psychological effect of this lengthening adolescence. However, again, it is not our job as teachers and educators to be experts on the 'why?' part of this. The statistics show that this is the case, and so it is our responsibility to respond appropriately and consider this to be another factor in the evolving nature of RSE. Physiological evolution, as well as the changing nature of sexual interactions as technology continues to advance, and the ever-changing nature of society mean that RSE must keep with the times and be relevant for the generation we are educating. Also to be considered when teaching any subject is what a lengthened period of adolescence means for the abilities of our students and how we might adapt to support them. We've mentioned the exhaustion. Other symptoms can be a lapse in concentration, feeling over- or under-stimulated, unexpected sexual arousal, mood swings and flashes of anxiety, anger, sadness, jealousy. There's so much going on and we expect this age group to sit exams, perform in sports, compete in arts, be social and spend quality family time, and it does not end there. We want adolescents to make rational, level-headed and ethically balanced decisions about sexual activity and relationships, with no real education in doing so, at the same time as hormones are coursing through their bodies sending a million different messages through every fibre of their weary being. Karim describes his avoidance of sexual relationships at this stage in life:

> I never had a girlfriend in my teen years as I felt very uncomfortable with the whole boyfriend/girlfriend thing. I distanced myself from this by throwing myself fully into a gender-neutral sport so that I didn't have to associate with either groups of boys or girls, or feel the pressure of needing to date as I could always say that I had no time due to training, or had a competition coming up. It was a good escape from what was unknown and stressful to me. Well, nobody teaches you how to handle that stuff . . . you know . . . it's confusing. (Karim, age 22)

'Uncomfortable . . . distanced . . . pressure . . . escape . . . unknown . . . stressful . . . confusing' – recognising these stressors and teaching young people what to expect during adolescence can help a lot. Providing structure, as well as autonomy, is also invaluable. Puberty can be frightening as the human body does lots of things that feel alien. It's natural to feel out of control. To be able to get a sense of autonomy back, through formal and structured learning about real relationships, real sex, real people and all the many versions of normal life on this planet can be of great comfort and relief.

At this level, what we'd expect to see in RSE is:

- What is sex and what does it mean? Beliefs, ethics, morality, boundaries and learning to communicate those clearly.
- A discussion of glossary terms and using the knowledge in the room to talk about the language used around sex and the implications of that, in terms of respect.
- Internet safety around pornography, grooming, internet dating and relationships online (sexual and non-sexual).
- Defining LGBTQI+ as well as what it means to be heterosexual. Let's think about the assumptions people have about gender, age and sexuality when it comes to sex.

KEY STAGE 4 SEX EDUCATION (AGE 14–16 YEARS)

As we have implicitly suggested, sex education needs to occur during the earlier key stages, so that by the time a student is in Key Stage 4, they have a solid foundation and many of the areas have been covered. It would be worth consolidating previous coverage and inviting students to identify areas they wish to be covered to provide a sense of autonomy and self-determination in their learning. They could contribute to a resource bank for younger years, for example. However, if you are currently working with Key Stage 4, you may find that students have had limited experience of sex education in the previous Key Stages. As such, we would encourage you to find out what has been covered, and to adapt and use guidance provided in this book for your class. Indeed, this may similarly apply if you teach in any of the other Key Stages.

Once satisfied that Key Stage 4 students have covered the content in Lessons in Love & Understanding in the order we suggest, there is a level of sex education that is important to address in keeping with trends of the times and the emergence of sexual practices becoming more commonplace with today's young people. As we have previously mentioned, the world of online pornography, internet sex and mobile phone dating is bringing a wider variety of possibilities to watch or engage in sexual acts with others online, either by arranging to meet in person or through sex play via webcam, chat room, etc. Safety and boundaries around arranging any type of meeting with strangers are paramount, especially where sex is concerned. The knowledge within the class can be very useful in thinking about potential problems and how those might be averted.

For this age group, it is helpful to look into different types of sexual play. We've spoken about sexual desire in terms of who one might be attracted to. With this age group, we can explore more explicitly what some people enjoy doing. You can imagine already the types of jokes that this topic will raise if they are not handled with great care (animals and other students' mothers are typically mentioned at some point as standard Key Stage 4 banter). It is best to have a number of areas that you ask pupils to explore in groups and talk about the various concepts, and pros and cons. This is pulling on perspective (Lessons in Love & Understanding 1) and thinking about what certain sexual play might achieve for someone engaging in it, as well as what might be considered less or undesirable. Examples might be **BDSM**, role play, **orgy**, chemsex, and anything else that a student might suggest, even if you've never heard of it. It's good to build a collective definition of what the practice involves, and then to think about how the people involved safely set the boundaries for what they consent to engage with. For example, BDSM normally includes 'safe words' that are pre-agreed so that there is a clear exit should one wish to end the action. With role play, improvisation might be agreed on or a fantasy scenario discussed upfront. If there are people in existing relationships within an orgy, perhaps they have agreed rules about sexual acts that are or aren't allowed with others outside the relationship. Or for chemsex, prior consideration at reducing associated risks, such as safe-sex packs and choosing trusted partners, might be factored in. Other hot topics are the age-old concerns such as the sex industry and prostitution, unplanned pregnancy, STIs and sexual assault. Avoiding these issues will not make them go away. By facilitating discussions in the classroom, we can help young people make informed choices about sex and also help them know what to do if they run into problems (see Additional reading in Chapter 8).

At Key Stage 4 the pressure is on. What we would expect to cover is:

- Everything that should have been done in the previous Key Stages, hopefully as a repeat, but some of this material may be for the first time.
- Respect, consent and considering one's own values, beliefs and identity as well as honouring those of others.
- Different types of sex and sexual acts: boundaries, contracting and safety.
- Considering what 'good sex' might mean, from different perspectives.

Notice that we haven't mentioned LGBTQI+ by this time, as we trust that equality and diversity are so fully imbedded in your practice that there is no need for us to remind you or your students.

CONCLUSION

In this chapter, sexuality has been explored from introducing the interplay of social identity, behaviour/practices and fantasy/desire. We use this model to help students understand themselves and those around them from both an interpersonal and relational perspective, and also to appreciate that sexuality is individualised. We look at the safeguarding aspects of sex education. At Key Stage 1, this is in promoting autonomy and facilitating students to take ownership of their bodies, and also preventing shame and protecting dignity. By Key Stage 2, we are focusing on puberty, adolescence and the complex mix of associated physiological and psychological effects. We are teaching about variations within healthy development and the many different versions of normal that exist in terms of thoughts, feelings and emotions during adolescence. Sexual intercourse and safe sex may be introduced at this stage or at Key Stage 3, but at whatever stage it is decided to introduce both, this must be inclusive of LGBTQI+ as well as multi-faith communities. Of course, throughout this book we assume that as teachers and educators you also make this appropriately accessible for young people with all levels of SEND. By Key Stages 3 and 4, sex education needs to be relevant to the world of relationships and sex in which those teenagers are living. This involves teachers learning from the knowledge in the room, and facilitating group work in order to research and address topical issues and the real concerns facing the modern generation as they embark on adulthood.

KEY POINTS

- Sexuality comprises social identity, behaviour/practice and fantasy/desire.
- The counterparts of sexual identity may vary in size, with one being more or less dominant than the others.
- It is not difficult to adapt existing RSE packages and the way your school currently operates to teach in an all-inclusive way.
- Sex education must be relevant and represent the reality of the world, and cover the various challenges and pressures faced by young people today.
- Specific Key Stage guidance exists as we have outlined in this and other chapters.

LESSONS IN LOVE & UNDERSTANDING 4: SEXUALITY AND SEX

(For the RSE teaching that we advocate, 4-year-olds can be included in the KS1 learning and 17-year-olds can be included in the KS4 learning.)

KS1 (AGE 5–7 YEARS)

- If your class is not already doing this, massage can not only be taught as an exercise in promoting positive therapeutic and stress-reducing touch, but it is also an opportunity for children to practise using their boundaries. They must ask permission to massage and the recipient chooses to allow or not, which is then respectfully accepted. Reinforcing these boundaries and the need for permission to touch anybody is an important early lesson and offers autonomy and respect to both sides of the relationship (see Additional reading at the end of the chapter).

(Continued)

- Discuss the non-sexual functions of various parts of the body and introduce the idea of healthy bodies and looking after our bodies. This can be everything from personal hygiene, healthy eating, exercise, sunshine, etc. Talk about the process of fuelling our bodies and using the toilet. Discuss genitalia and keeping privates private.

- Make your own Happy Families cards. These should consist of a mixture of roles that can be identified as a group by having a rhyming sound – e.g. Mr Lake, Mr Rake, Miss Drake, Baby Blake or Mrs Danning, Mx Manning and Baby Channing. Hand out the cards randomly to the class and then they must say their name while listening out for their rhyming family group. They must stand together with their group with any baby in the family sitting on the floor by their feet. The slowest family to form are eliminated from the game and the cards are handed out again at random; repeat until there is one winning family remaining. This is a great team-work game and a nice visual of changing families and cooperation.

KS2 (AGE 7–11 YEARS)

- A biology lesson on anatomy including genitalia and a focus on puberty with what can be expected during human development. This should include photographs of non-air-brushed normal bodies at different stages of puberty representing a variety of race, shapes, sizes, disability, body hair, and skin characters. This should be for mixed gender. It is not helpful to keep menstruation a secret from boys or wet dreams hidden from girls. This secrecy implies that natural bodily functions are something to be ashamed of. Normalising is key here. Reproduction should be taught with the clear understanding that there are various ways that people become parents, irrespective of their gender, age, fertility situation, relationship status, etc.

- Give the class a creative exercise where they imagine they are speaking for their body. They can make a letter, poster or a rule sheet, requesting how they (as their body) would like to be treated. Ask them to consider all areas of respect such as healthy eating, hygiene, exercise, drinking water and keeping safe. The body perhaps likes cuddles from trusted people, or maybe does not like to be touched. It might like to be a certain temperature and get a certain amount of sleep. In pairs, the class can practise telling one another what their body needs to affirm those healthy ideas and work on clear communication of boundaries.

- Understanding sex. Why might people choose to have sex? Assess all the possibilities and think about reasons that they may choose not to. Look at the legal age for having consensual sex and discuss sexual relationships and the different things that might mean.

KS3 (AGE 11–14 YEARS)

- What ideas do we have around sex? Where did these come from? Have five posters for the class to work on giving answers under each category: parents/family, school/teachers, faith/religious groups, media/internet, friends/peers. Bring this to a group discussion about similarities and differences in our ideas. Do our ideas represent a wide proportion of society? Provide resources for safe research on **sexual health**.
- Safe sex – and what this means. Let's consider choices and different ways in which people have sexual contact. Lists of pros and cons in terms of safety. Condoms, **lubes, dental dams**. STIs, what to do if something goes wrong.
- Generation porn. Online sex and relationships. Sharing of pornography, **sexting**, trading, online dating. Lesson on the psychological effects of pornography, positive and negative. What type of relationships do we see in pornography? Are Heterosexual and LGBTQI+ people represented in a realistic way?

KS4 (AGE 14–16 YEARS)

- Safe sex – what this means, live and online. Fetish, voyeur/exhibitionist, BDSM, **kink**, chemsex and other types of sexual practice. Boundaries and safety: this is a great lesson to plan as safety and boundaries are key to many of these practices, and they are dependent on trust and mutual consent and responsibility.
- A prerequisite to pleasure: consider from various perspectives, what might be the conditions to allow satisfying sex? This can be via case studies.
- For both Key Stages 3 and 4, a highly recommended documentary is *Sex in Class* (Channel 4) in which sexologist Goedele Liekens demonstrates how sex education can be taught properly. As the review

(Continued)

for the documentary from *The Radio Times* reported, 'Sex education is not an optional extra to be awkwardly bumbled through by teachers and students. When taught properly, it can change lives.'

In Chapter 7, we consider good practice and how to set up a safe space for you to deliver these lessons.

ADDITIONAL READING

KS1 (AGE 5–7 YEARS)

- *Everywhere Babies* by Susan Meyers.
- *We Chose You* by Tony and Lauren Dungy.
- *A Mother for Choco* by Keiko Kasza.
- *My Body! What I Say Goes!* by Jayneen Sanders.
- *My Underpants Rule!* by Kate and Rod Power.
- *No Means No!* by Jayneen Sanders.

KS2 (AGE 7–11 YEARS)

- *It's Perfectly Normal* by Robie H. Harris and Michael Emberley.
- *Some Secrets Should Never Be Kept* by Jayneen Sanders.
- *The Moon Within* by Aida Salazar.
- *Dazzling Travis: A Story About Being Confident & Original* by Hannah Carmona Dias.

KS3/4 (AGE 11–16 YEARS)

- *This Book is Gay* by Juno Dawson.
- *The ABC's of LGBT+* by Ashley Mardell.
- *The Vagina Monologues* by Eve Ensler.
- *Yay! You're Gay! Now What?* by Riyadh Khalaf.
- *Sex is a Funny Word: A Book About Bodies, Feelings and You* by Cory Silverberg and Fiona Smyth.

ADULTS

- *The ABC's of LGBT+* by Ashley Mardell.
- *Great Relationships and Sex Education: 200+ Activities for Educators Working with Young People* by Alice Hoyle and Ester McGeeney.

5

GENDER AND SEXOLOGY THROUGH THE AGES

CONTENTS

- Why this chapter?
- Timeline
- Hate crimes
- The significance of Stonewall
- Section 28
- Putting this in context within schools
- Conclusion

OBJECTIVES

- To be aware that the history surrounding gender and sexology is as old as civilisation.
- To understand key developments affecting gender and sexology.
- To appreciate the continued suppression of gender and sexology.
- To understand what is meant by a bias incident and a hate crime.
- To understand the significance of Section 28 and how this has reso-nated through schools to today.

WHY THIS CHAPTER?

While the initial chapters have provided a model for relationships and sex education, it would be useful to highlight the development of key themes to demonstrate how concepts of gender and sexuality have evolved before we progress to the later chapters which explore how to embed RSE purposefully into your school. Some of the themes in this we may deem to be different from our societal norms, espe-cially if they are from a different millennium and culture (of course, we have questioned 'what is normal?', or 'is my normal your normal?'), yet the main theme of this chapter is to highlight how oppression and repression has been applied and experienced by many, while also incorporating moments of celebration – for example, the advances in fertility treatment. While homosexual men are no longer executed in the UK (as they were prior to 1861), the rise of **hate crime**, from the low level, such as swearing or name calling, to 'kerbing' and murder, is on the increase. Reading this chapter may be upsetting: it was not pleasant to write, neither do we think it will be easy to read.

As with the subjects of all the chapters, a book or several volumes could be written for each. This chapter is no different. Consequently, there will be areas, examples and case studies we have omitted; how-ever, we hope that the chapter provides a glimpse across a range of areas such as the legal, sexuality, trans and hate crime timelines to enable you to investigate further.

From an educational perspective, the information provided in this chapter may help to facilitate discussions, such as whether there are gender-specific toys and games, the inclusion of transgender athletes in sport, the portrayal of sex, sexuality, body image and stereotypes in the media, through to an historical perspective on advocacy, acceptance and inclusion. Fundamental to this chapter, however, is how the individual sense of self has been supressed and oppressed, and this is detrimental to any student who just wants to learn and be who they are.

TIMELINE

UPPER PALAEOLITHIC

28,000 BCE Many societies globally had fertility symbols, such as the Venus of Willendorf, a Venus figurine found in Austria.

NEOLITHIC

8000 BCE The Sans rock paintings in Zimbabwe depict homosexuality.

7000 BCE Images that depict individuals with female breasts and male genitals appeared in burials or religious settings around the Mediterranean area.

CHALCOLITHIC (COPPER AGE)

3500 BCE Sumerian and Akkadian texts highlighted transgender priests.

BRONZE AGE

2400 BCE The first same-sex male couple in history were recorded – Khnumhotep and Niankhkhnum, two Ancient Egyptian royal servants.

570 BCE The poet Sappho died. She was famous for her lesbian themes within her poems. She was exiled from her homeland, the island of Lesbos, Greece, in 600 BCE.

400–200 BCE The *Kama Sutra* was compiled by the Indian philosopher, Vātsyāyana.

IRON AGE

AD54 Nero conducted a legal marriage ceremony between two men, Pythagoras and Sporus.

EARLY/HIGH MIDDLE AGES

654 The first European secular law to criminalise homosexuality was introduced by the Visigothic kingdom.

1140 The Benedictine monk, Gratian, introduced the concept of marriage as consent between two people in his canon law textbook.

1179 The Third Lateran Council of Rome issued a decree to excommunicate anyone engaged in sodomy.

LATE MIDDLE AGES

1275 The Statutes of Westminster ruled that sexual intercourse with a girl 'within age' (under the marital age of 12) was illegal.

1260 In the kingdom of France, those who were caught as first offending sodomites lost their **testicles**. For a second offence, they lost their penis. They were punished for a third offence by being burned alive. Women caught in lesbian acts were similarly mutilated and burned.

1447 Jean d'Arc (also known as 'Joan of Arc') was burned at the stake for heresy, specifically due to her purported relapse by dressing as a man (which was originally for pragmatic battlefield purposes, but also to prevent her being **raped** by her guards in prison). The clothing relapse, although a marginal offence, was one that would subsequently incur the death penalty. The trial records indicate that she was provided only with male clothing by her English guards, which helped to seal the verdict.

1500s

1549 Marriage vows were written by Thomas Cranmer in the *Book of Common Prayer*.

1532 The Holy Roman Empire imposed the death penalty for sodomy.

1533 King Henry VIII passed the 'Buggery Act of England'. Anal intercourse and zoophilia (sexual fixation on non-human animals) were punishable by hanging.

1553 Mary Tudor repealed all laws that were passed by Henry VIII.

1563 Elizabeth I re-enacted the Buggery Act.

1563 Marriage was officially deemed one of the seven sacraments within Catholicism by the Council of Trent.

1700s

1711 Joseph-François Lafitau spent six years living among the Iroquois Native American tribe and reported their transgender roles.

1753 The Clandestine Marriage Act required couples to get married in a church or chapel by a minister.

1791 France decriminalised homosexuality.

1800s

1835 James Pratt and John Smith were executed at Newgate Prison by hanging. They are the last known executions for homosexuality in Great Britain.

1836 The Marriage Act allowed non-religious civil marriages to be conducted in registry offices.

1843 Dr Martin Barry discovered the link between spermatozoa fertilising the ovum and pregnancy.

1861 The sentence of sodomy was reduced from execution to imprisonment for either ten years or life (1861 Offences Against the Person Act, UK).

1882 The diaphragm (or 'Occlusive Pessary') was invented by Dr Wilhelm Mensinga.

1885 The age of consent was raised to under 13 as a felony and a misdemeanour for 13–16 years of age.

1889 The first sex education course at a British school is run by Cecil Reddie at Abbotsholme School, near Rocester in Staffordshire.

1890 *The Picture of Dorian Gray*, written by Oscar Wilde, was published in *Lippincott's Monthly Magazine*, although it received harsh criticism for its homosexual allusions and decadence.

1890 Homosexuality was legalised by the Vatican.

1892 The term 'heterosexual' was first published in C.G. Chaddock's translation of *Psychopathia Sexualis* by Kafft-Ebing.

1895 The Marquess of Queensbury disapproved of the relationship between his son, Lord Alfred (also known as 'Bosie'), and Oscar Wilde. Queensbury accused Oscar Wilde of being a sodomite. Wilde sued Queensbury for criminal libel. Wilde lost the case as evidence demonstrated that he had used male prostitutes. Wilde was required to pay Queensbury's expenses, which in turn led to his bankruptcy. Wilde was subsequently arrested on charges of sodomy and **gross indecency**. In May, he was sentenced to hard labour in Pentonville Prison; he was then moved to Wandsworth Prison where he collapsed due to illness and hunger. He was transferred to Reading jail in November.

1900s

1901 Havelock Ellis published *Studies in the Psychology of Sex*, which suggested that women do enjoy sex and that homosexuality is an inherent trait.

1905 Nettie Stevens, a geneticist who researched beetles, suggested that sex was determined by the X and Y chromosomes.

1910 Dr Magnus Hirschfeld distinguished the terms '**transvestite**' and 'transgender'.

1916 Margaret Sanger established the first birth control clinic in New York. However, she was arrested ten days later and imprisoned for a month.

1917 Dr Alan L. Hart became the first person to have sexual reassignment surgery, having a **hysterectomy** and gonadectomy.

1919 Magnus Hirschfeld established The Institute for Sexology in Berlin, a multi-agency institute consisting of doctors, psychiatrists, marriage counsellors, and so forth. It was destroyed by the Nazis in 1933.

1919 Frederick Kilian developed the latex condom. They had previously been made from rubber, animal skins, cloth and even horn.

1920s

1920s The 'rhythm method' of contraception was developed by Japanese and Australian scientists.

1928 Virginia Woolf published *Orlando*, a novel that follows a person through time and between genders.

1930s

1930 Lili Elbe, a Danish artist, travelled to Germany for the first of four sex reassignment surgeries. She died a year later due to her body's rejection of an implanted uterus.

1937 The Nazis used an inverted pink triangle to identify gay men in concentration camps.

1938 The USA decriminalised birth control.

1939 The word 'gay' was used for the first time with reference to homosexuality.

1940s

1945 The first **female to male** sex reassignment surgery by Sir Harold Gillies and Ralph Millard in the UK.

1948–54 Dr Alfred Kinsey published a series of reports on sexuality within society.

1949 Hormones were first used for transgender individuals in San Francisco by Harry Benjamin.

1950s

1952 Christine Jorgensen underwent sex reassignment surgery which was widely publicised in the *New York Daily News*, which in turn raised the profile of transgender.

1952 Alan Turing, the developer of the 'Bombe' (more commonly known as the Enigma codebreaker machine), was prosecuted for 'gross indecency' and fired from his job. Turing accepted '**chemical castration**' to avoid imprisonment.

1953 Hugh Hefner published the first edition of *Playboy* magazine featuring Marilyn Monroe on the front cover.

1957 The Wolfenden Report was presented to the UK Government, recommending that homosexual behaviour between consenting adults in private should not be a crime. It took a further ten years for the law to be changed.

1960s

1960 John Cremin was murdered by Antony Miller in Queen's Park, Glasgow, having been a victim of a homophobic attack by Douglas Denovan and Tony Miller. Miller was the last person to be hanged in Scotland.

1966 The Beaumont Society was founded in the UK to provide support for the trans community.

1967 'The 'Sexual Offences Act' allowed private consensual sex between men aged over 21 years in England and Wales.

1969 The 'Campaign for Homosexual Equality' was formed in the UK to campaign for law reform, and better medical and social support for LGBTQI+ people.

1969 The first 'Stonewall Riot' took place in New York on 28 June.

1970s

1970 In April, the first Pride march took place in New York to commemorate the anniversary of the Stonewall Riots.

1970 The first Pride march in the UK took place in Highbury Fields, London.

1971 The term 'transgender' was first used.

1973 *Playgirl* magazine was first published.

1977 Harvey Milk was the first openly gay politician in the USA. He was elected to office in San Francisco in 1977. He was murdered on 27 November the following year.

1978 The first baby was born from **in vitro fertilisation (IVF)**.

1978 Harvey Milk asked Gilbert Baker to design a symbol of gay pride. The colours of the rainbow flag represent the diversity of the LGBTQI+ community.

1980s

1980 The Sexual Offences Act was extended to Scotland, decriminalising homosexuality.

1980 The Standards of Care were established by the Harry Benjamin International Gender Dysphoria Association.

1981 The USA reported that there were 270 cases of gay men with AIDS, of which 121 had died. Over 35 million people have died from **HIV** and currently, there are 36 million people living with the disease.

1982 Terrence Higgins became one of the first British men to die from AIDS.

1985 HIV testing began in the UK.

1988 1 December was designated World **AIDS** Day.

1988 The UK Government introduced Section 28, which stated that local government should not 'promote the teaching of the acceptability of homosexuality as a pretend family relationship'.

1989 Stonewall, a leading advocacy group in the UK, was formed. It was established on 24 May 1989 at Sir Ian McKellen's house, one year to the day after the introduction of Section 28.

1990s

1991 Freddie Mercury, the lead singer of Queen, died of an AIDS-related illness, aged 45.

1991 The red ribbon was first used as a symbol to campaign against HIV/AIDS.

1993 Ireland decriminalised homosexuality.

1993 Brandon Teena, a **trans man**, was gang raped and murdered in Nebraska, aged 21.

1994 The Criminal Justice and Public Order Act (UK) lowered the age of homosexual consent to 18.

1998 Mathew Shepard was beaten, then tied to a fence in Wyoming in a homophobic attack. He was discovered after 18 hours but died six days later in hospital, aged 21.

1998 Rita Hester was murdered at her home in Boston in a transphobic attack. This was the catalyst for the Transgender Day of Remembrance, which is commemorated annually on 20 November.

1999 The Admiral Duncan, a gay pub in Soho, was bombed by David Copeland. Three people were killed and 70 injured.

1999 The Sex Discrimination Act in the UK was amended to protect individuals on the basis of gender reassignment.

2000s

2000 Scotland repeals Section 28 on 21 June.

2000 The Sexual Offences (Amendment) Act of 2000 lowered the age of homosexual consent to 16.

2000 The Sexual Offences (Amendment) Act of 2000 stated that the age of consent for penetrative sex, **oral sex** and mutual masturbation is 16 years of age, regardless of sexual orientation. If a person is under age 18, the maximum prison sentence is 5 years; if they are over 18, the offender may receive up to 14 years.

2001 The Netherlands was the first country to introduce equal marriage between any two people.

2003 Section 28 was repealed in England.

2004 The Gender Recognition Act (2004) became law.

2005 The Civil Partnership Act (2004) was passed, an Act that gave same-sex couples the right to enter into **civil partnerships** and receive similar rights to heterosexual couples.

2010s

2013 Nikki Sinclaire became the first openly transgender Member of Parliament.

2014 The United Nations Human Rights Council adopted a landmark resolution for LGBTQI+ rights, condemning violence and discrimination based on sexual orientation or gender identity across the globe. During the vote, 25 countries voted in favour, 14 against and 7 abstained.

2014 The Marriage (Same-Sex Couples) Act (2013) was passed on 13 March. The first same-sex marriages were able to take place from 29 March onwards.

2014 Scotland introduced equal marriage.

2015 Caitlyn Jenner was the first transgender woman to appear on the cover of *Vanity Fair* magazine.

2016 During a shooting at Pulse, a gay bar and nightclub in Orlando, 49 people were killed and 53 were injured.

2018 The Vatican used the acronym 'LGBT' for the first time in an official document.

2020 Northern Ireland legalised equal marriage on 13 January.

Please note: more detailed timelines that will be kept up to date are available on www.lessonsinlove.info

COMMENT

From the timeline above, there are some themes that may be identified. For 10,000 years, evidence of gay and lesbian relationships have been recorded, and for 9,000 years, there has been evidence of trans individuals. Yet a parallel timeline has also been evidenced: that of the stigma, isolation, hate, lack of acceptance and levels of violence experienced by those who are deemed different from the prevalent trends in society.

HATE CRIMES

According to Stonewall (Bachmann and Gooch, 2017):

- 1 in 5 LGBTQI+ people have experienced a hate crime or incident because of their sexual orientation and/or gender identity in the last 12 months.
- 2 in 5 trans people have experienced a hate crime or incident because of their gender identity in the last 12 months.
- 4 in 5 anti-LGBTQI+ hate crimes and incidents go unreported, with younger LGBTQI+ people particularly reluctant to go to the police.
- There has been a 78% increase in hate crime for LGBTQI+ people from 2013 to 2017.
- 28% of LGBTQI+ people who visited a faith service or place of worship in the past 12 months have experienced discrimination.

The University of Leicester's Centre for Hate Studies (2019) provides additional statistics:

- 88% of LGBTQI+ people who have experienced hate crime have been left with emotional and physical scars.

- Only 14% of LGBTQI+ victims reported their most recent experience of hate crime to the police.
- Victims of **transphobia** can be targeted up to 50 times per year with only 3 in 10 reporting any incidents.

Unfortunately, accurate numbers are not possible to ascertain due to the number of crimes which go unreported, along with the lack of statistics of gender and sexual identity. However, as a comparison to other hate crimes, a report by Allen and Zayed (2019) for the House of Commons Library Briefing Paper, Number 08537 reported that in 2015/16:

- 101,000 hate crimes were reported in relation to race, notably with 1.1% of Asian/Asian British adults aged over 16 years experiencing hate crime, and a total of 3.2% of British adults experiencing a hate crime in relation to their ethnic group.
- 39,000 hate crimes were reported in relation to religion, notably with 1.5% of Muslim British adults aged over 16 years experiencing a hate crime, and a total of 3% of British adults experiencing a hate crime based on their religion.
- 30,000 hate crimes were reported in relation to sexual orientation. This is approximately 40% of the 108,100 responses to the National LGBTQI+ Survey in 2018, with trans people twice as likely to experience threats of physical assault or sexual harassment (11%) compared to 5% of the LGBTQI+ community as a whole.
- 52,000 hate crimes were reported in relation to disability, including 79% of parents of a disabled child having had offensive comments aimed towards them or their child either directly in person, or through social media.

At the time of going to press, the Home Office (2019) have provided updated research: sexual orientation hate crime has increased from 2017/18 to 2018/19 by 25% with 14,491 reported incidents while trans hate crimes have increased in the same period by 27% with 2,333 reported incidents. Of such crimes, 54% are public order, while 26% are crimes against the person.

A hate incident can take numerous forms – for example, name calling, physical abuse (such as hitting, pushing, spitting, an object being thrown), verbal abuse, threats of violence, harassment, bullying, harm or damage to personal property, and so forth. Within the UK, the police and Crown Prosecution Service have defined hate incidents according to whether the victim or anyone else think that the hostility or prejudice was based on disability, race, religion, transgender identity, or sexual orientation. Furthermore, anyone can be a victim of a hate incident – for example, if a person has been targeted because they were perceived to be a gay man.

A hate incident becomes a hate crime if a law is broken, such as physical or sexual assault, criminal damage, harassment, theft, fraud, hate mail (under the Malicious Communications Act, 1988), or through causing harassment, alarm or distress (Public Order Act, 1986). If a crime is judged to have been a hate crime, the judge can impose a tougher sentence under the Criminal Justice Act, 2003.

Hate crimes (predominantly against the LGBTQI+ community) have been perpetuated for millennia, initially through societal or religious systems resulting in castration, mutilation or execution. With the advancing of civilisation, the type of hate crime has changed and sadly this remains explicit across any street, screen, school or staffroom in the UK.

THE SIGNIFICANCE OF STONEWALL

During the 1960s in the USA and across other countries, protests were rife: from President Kennedy's assassination, to the assassinations of Martin Luther King and Bobby Kennedy, riots in Paris by students, through to protests against the Vietnam War and the throwing of bras into bins (not burning bras as commonly thought) in protests against the Miss America pageant, change was occurring. One building that was a catalyst for change was the Stonewall Inn, New York.

The Stonewall Inn was a bar in Greenwich Village, run by the Mafia. Greenwich Village became a location for gay men and lesbian women to settle and the Stonewall Inn had been redeveloped to become a private members club due to the prohibition of alcohol sales. The club was the only bar in New York City where gay men could dance, although the club also attracted transvestites, the homeless, and an even racial mix between Hispanic, black and white clients. The police raided the bar regularly, although they normally provided a tip-off beforehand and received bribes from the Mafia for superficial raids.

As a result of the Mafia increasing the amounts extorted from wealthier customers, and with the police receiving little of this extra illicit income, law enforcement attempted to raid the bar with a view of closing it down in the early hours of 28 June 1976. During the raid, the police were more heavy-handed than usual. The police requested additional vans for arrested customers, while those who were released congregated outside the front door. The crowd started to grow more hostile, especially when one of the police officers pushed a **trans woman**, Tammy Novak, who responded by hitting the officer with her handbag; the officer then hit Novak around her head with his baton. During this time, a lesbian woman, Stormé DeLarverie, resisted being arrested. She shouted to the crowd, 'Why don't you guys do something?', which resulted in a full riot. According to Todd (2019), the riot was predominantly led by the most marginalised: trans people, people of colour, women perceived as '**butch**', men perceived as 'effeminate' and homeless youngsters. Rioting continued for a second night and periodically until the following Wednesday. The riots led to more protests and the establishment of advocacy groups internationally.

To commemorate the Stonewall Riots, a year after the initial rioting, the Christopher Street Liberation Day was held in New York, with similar Gay Pride marches taking place in Los Angeles and Chicago. By 1971, Gay Pride marches had been established in other US cities, Paris, Stockholm, West Berlin and London.

SECTION 28

LGBTQI+ students did not exist for 5,657 days (15 years, 5 months and 26 days) between 1988 and 2003. Well, of course they did, but not in the eyes of the UK Parliament. Being gay was a choice according to the Prime Minister at the time, who introduced a damning piece of legislation, Section 28.

Section 28 (also known as Clause 28) of the Local Government Act 1988 included the addition of Section 21 to the Local Government Act 1986. Specifically, this piece of legislation stated:

A Local Authority shall not:

a) Intentionally promote homosexuality or publish material with the intention of promoting homosexuality.

   b) Promote the teaching in any maintained school of the acceptability of homosexuality as a pretended family relationship.

Nothing above shall be taken to prohibit the doing of anything for the purpose of treating or preventing the spread of disease.

It is important to note that the legislation only focused on homo-sexuality and not transgender. However, by extension, any discussion about LGBTQI+ was silenced.

Section 28 was instigated for a range of possible reasons. During the early 1980s, AIDS became a dominant headline and it was popularly reported that it was spread by gay men and lesbian women. Many myths surrounded AIDS as it was a relatively unknown disease with no cure. Some religious people considered the disease to be a punishment for the behaviour of lesbian women and gay men; television advertis-ments were dark and foreboding. In 1983, the British Social Attitudes Survey reported that 62% of respondents reported that 'Sexual rela-tions between two adults of the same sex' was 'always wrong' or 'mostly wrong'. This rose to 75% by 1987, although by 2012 it had fallen to 28%. Additionally, the 1980s were a politically turbulent time with high unemployment, rioting and large-scale social changes, among many other factors. It was perceived that anything residing from the previous Labour Government was the 'Loony Left', particularly with hubs such as the Inner London Education Authority (ILEA), which was run by Labour. Furthermore, the Greater London Council (GLC) had provided significant funding to LGBTQI+ groups at a time when the public were very sensitive about their money for 'rates' (or, as it is called today, 'Council Tax') being used to fund such organisations.

A common perception was that such schools were challenging the concept of the family consisting of a mummy and daddy as being outdated, along with books that children were bringing home from school such as *Jenny Lives with Eric and Martin*, that Labour wanted *Young, Gay and Proud* to be read in schools, and other books such as *The Milkman's on his Way* and *Police Out of School, 1985*.

During the 1987 Conservative Party Conference in Blackpool, the Prime Minister, Margaret Thatcher, announced, 'Children who need to be taught to respect traditional moral values are being taught that they have an inalienable right to be gay . . . . All of those children are being cheated of a sound start in life. Yes, cheated.'

Despite many protests being held, very few were covered on the news. As a result, protesters developed innovative strategies. During the evening that Section 28 was being voted on in the House of Lords, six lesbian protesters, orchestrated by Sally Francis, got into the public gallery. Three protesters abseiled into the House of Lords from the public gallery when the vote had finished. Furthermore, protesters disrupted the BBC's *Six O' Clock News*, where one protester handcuffed herself to a TV camera and another to the news desk. Another, Booan Temple, was rugby tackled to the ground and dragged away.

As mentioned in the timeline in this chapter, a year to the day after the introduction of Section 28, Stonewall was established by 14 founders. The charity has been successful in lobbying Parliament for the repeal of Section 28, the recognition of LGBT hate crimes through the Criminal Justice Act 2003 and the introduction of the Civil Partnership Act 2004, among other legislation.

While no prosecutions were ever made during this time, the fear of teachers mentioning homosexuality and the culture of fear that presided in schools was profound. According to the NUT, professional judgement was directly influenced with the fear of prosecution, also that schools felt powerless to challenge homophobic bullying. Furthermore, teachers were fearful of being 'outed' for their gender or sexual identity. If a teacher transitioned, this would be reported in newspapers.

With the increased criticisms and protests about RSE 2020, along with the shadow of Section 28, teachers who identified as LGBTQI+ could be fearful of losing their jobs, specifically if they worked in faith schools, despite protection under the Equality Act 2010. Furthermore, the lasting implications are that even today, some teachers are fearful of teaching about same-sex relationships and feel that this should be avoided at all costs. However, there are students in most schools who may have same-sex parents or are aware of same-sex family relationships. Indeed, according to Stonewall, only 13% of students have been taught about how to be part of a healthy LGBTQI+ relationship. Consequently, for the past 30 years, the imposed or perceived limitations of discussing LGBTQI+ in school have directly affected numerous students. With recent protests against RSE 2020 and the climate of fear in schools still prevalent, we hope that this book may help in supporting schools and teachers to navigate new directions.

PUTTING THIS IN CONTEXT WITHIN SCHOOLS

While the timeline in this chapter has highlighted the interplay of sexuality, gender, medical advances in fertility treatment, the law, oppression and hate, we trust that the positive glimmers of light from the past few decades continue to brighten, not just to the point of acceptance or tolerance, but to celebrate every individual for who they are.

As teachers, our multifaceted roles are profound, and indeed, as teachers, we should enjoy that our profession is one where we can truly make societal changes, more so (we believe) than any other profession. From planting those seeds through to watering and nurturing the seedling, it may take time for our students to flourish. So while we take forward this celebration and nurturing of our students, our attention needs to be directed to the present. Where are we, what are our responsibilities and what are the next steps?

Thankfully, there are significant moves being made in this area. In 2017, the then Prime Minister Theresa May challenged society to 'Explain or Change'. The Department for Education along with the Chartered College of Teaching, teaching unions and other organisations provided a collective response, perhaps the most significant part of which is that provided by Dame Alison Peacock, CEO of the Chartered College of Teaching:

> The important role schools play in supporting community cohesion is needed now more than ever. With our communities becoming more diverse, schools need to reflect the areas where their pupils grow up. The positive impact of visible role models on young people from different backgrounds cannot be underestimated, it can help encourage pupils – no matter their ethnicity, gender or sexuality – to embrace who they are and be the best that they can be . . . . At the Chartered College we don't want to see the best teachers running into the closed doors of leadership because of their gender, ethnicity or sexuality. We want schools and pupils to benefit from teachers and leaders from all walks of life. (Department for Education, 2018)

In relation to RSE, the Angus Reid Publication Survey from 2011 explored adult respondents' reflections on learning about sex. The survey compared findings from Canada, Britain and the United States

(Canesco, 2011). From the results, the respondents from all three countries reported that learning from their friends was either very or moderately useful (67% in Britain), that the media was the next useful (65% in Britain), and that sex education lessons in school were only reported as very or moderately useful by 43% of respondents. It would appear that we are failing in sex education lessons, losing out to friends and the media. This is shocking. Given that the survey was conducted in 2011, how much more have the effects of social media impacted on the statistics?

In returning to our responsibilities as teachers, while we should all be engaged in relationships and sex education, our responsibilities are far broader, permeating every interaction with students. Responsibilities central to this are child protection and safeguarding. No doubt you maintain your professional development with a yearly refresher on safeguarding through staff development sessions or required eLearning courses.

Child protection and safeguarding are used interchangeably despite their differences. While child protection is the protection of children from violence, exploitation, abuse and neglect, safeguarding relates to the measures taken to protect the health, well-being and human rights of the individual. Safeguarding encompasses a wider range of issues, whereby a child's health and development should be prevented from harm by ensuring that the child grows up with the provision of safe and effective care. Consequently, not only is the focus on prevention and protection, but also on enabling children to flourish into adult life.

The core policies outlining the responsibilities within education are:

- The UN Convention on the Rights of the Child (Article 19).
- The Children Act 1989 (as amended).
- The Children and Social Work Act 2017.
- The Safeguarding Vulnerable Groups Act 2006.
- Working Together to Safeguard Children 2018.
- Keeping Children Safe in Education 2019.

While child protection and safeguarding deserve a chapter or even a book in their own right, we have taken the decision to trust that your school maintains its duty to keep staff informed and up to date with training. We will repeat this message twice in this next section: if you suspect that a student is at risk, contact your Designated Safeguarding

Lead (DSL) or your headteacher. Table 5.1 provides a summary of content related to this book despite acknowledging that different forms of abuse overlap, and also that the table is not designed to be an exhaustive list, just an indicator of areas.

Table 5.1 Summary of child protection and safeguarding content related to this book

Neglect	Physical indicators such as poor skin tone or hair tone, untreated medical conditions, unsuitable or inappropriate/inadequate clothing, obesity or lowweight, etc.
	Failing to supervise internet use, allowing access to pornography and other unsuitable materials.
	Behavioural indicators such as social isolation, consistent lateness, scrounging for food or equipment, other destructive tendencies.
Physical abuse	Causing physical harm to a child such as hitting, shaking, drowning, poisoning, burning, and so forth; also providing harmful substances such as alcohol or drugs to a child, or deliberately causing illness to a child.
	This may manifest in various ways such as unexplained injuries, bruises on soft body parts such as the stomach, cheeks, etc., keeping the child clothed to hide bruising or a fear of changing for PE, flinching from physical contact, and so forth.
Sexual abuse	Forcing or enticing a child to engage in sexual activity, with or without violence, and whether the child is aware or not of what is happening. This can be physical contact or non-physical such as exposing children to inappropriate images.
	According to the NSPCC (2019) an estimated 1 in 20 children in the UK have experienced **sexual abuse**.
	Sexual abuse characteristics include behavioural characteristics such as sexual behaviour inappropriate to the child's age, attempting to teach other peers about sexual activity, avoiding contact with other people, through to physical characteristics such as soiling undergarments and self-harming behaviours.
Grooming	This is the act of deliberately establishing a connection and subsequent trust with a child with the view to engage them in exploitation or sexual activity, often using threats or bribes.
	There can be an escalation of stages such as specifically targeting a child, establishing and gaining their trust, identifying a vulnerability, isolating the child, sexualising the relationship, maintaining control of the relationship.
Peer-on-peer abuse	Sexual harassment or sexual violence between two children of any age and sex. This is particularly prevalent for children identifying as LGBTQI+ or who may be perceived as LGBTQI+.
	Such abuse may include 'banter', sexual comments or jokes, or physical contact such as brushing past someone, upskirting photos, inappropriate touching of breasts, genitalia or buttocks, or interfering with someone's clothes such as flicking bras or lifting up skirts.
	Children deemed to have Specific Educational Needs or Disabilities are three times more likely to experience abuse than their peers.

(Continued)

Table 5.1 (Continued)

Child Sexual Exploitation (CSE)	According to the British Association of Social Workers (2018, p.6-7), over 4000 children are trafficked to the UK, and of these, approximately 26% are trafficked for child sexual exploitation. That is over a thousand children. Potential indicators of CSE are: disengagement from school, inappropriate sexual behaviour, unexplained gifts, changes in behaviour, having older girlfriends or boyfriends, etc.
Honour-based violence	This includes: **female genital mutilation (FGM)**, forced marriage, breast ironing, other forms of physical abuse outlined above, honour killings, forced suicide, psychological pressure such as humiliation and threats, and abandonment. In the UK, the NHS has reported 1,990 new cases of FGM in the first three months of 2019. Anyone who fails to protect a child from FGM could face seven years' imprisonment. Indicators of FGM are persistent or repeated absence, refusing to take part in PE or swimming lessons, difficulty sitting, standing or walking, behaviour changes such as depression or withdrawal.
Emotional abuse	The persistent emotional maltreatment of a child can have persistent and severe effects on a child's emotional development. The NSPCC (2016) reported that nearly 20,000 children experienced emotional abuse in 2016. Such abuse can include conveying to a child that they are worthless, useless, unloved or inadequate in some other way; it may involve hearing or seeing ill-treatment of another individual (such as a parent if a child lives in a split family); inappropriate expectations imposed on a child, etc. Indicators include: self-harm, delays in intellectual or physical development, negative comments about themselves, social isolation, fearfulness, and hyper-vigilant behaviour.

A fantastic resource that has recently been developed is the Traffic Light Tool developed by Brook (2019), an organisation that supports and advises on sexual health and well-being for the under-25s. The Traffic Light Tool provides green, amber and red behaviours for specific age groups (https://legacy.brook.org.uk/our-work/the-sexual-behaviours-traffic-light-tool). The tool is an easily accessible reference guide that helps to further contextualise in the classroom behaviours that may be exhibited and when to seek support. Please remember, if you suspect that a student is at risk, contact your Designated Safeguarding Lead (DSL) or your headteacher.

CONCLUSION

There have been historical accounts of different gender and sexual identities for at least 10,000 years. Although at different times and in different cultures this has been accepted, a twist of the historical lens has criminalised such identities. The Visigoths appear to be 500 years ahead of the Vatican in criminalising sodomy. However, the Vatican decriminalised homosexuality in 1890, 77 years before it was legalised in the UK. The past 100 years have advanced research and medical intervention to realign gender. As such, transgender is not a modern phenomenon despite the increased prevalence on social media. Through such a timeline, and with a liberal interpretation, we could argue that a historical figure such as Mary Tudor was one of the first LGBT advocates, although it has really been the last 150 years of advocacy that has brought about gradual change.

Unfortunately, such changes in society have taken longer with the increased prevalence of hate crime. How many more people will be killed either legally (because some countries still have the death penalty for homosexuality) or illegally? How many more children will experience hate incidents in UK schools today based on their race, religion, disability, sexual identity or gender identity? Is there a student in your class too afraid to speak out about their identity who is suffering inner turmoil? Is there a student who just wants to learn and be allowed to be who they are?

While empathy or sympathy are not required from society, equal respect is in order to allow the self to flourish. Such equal respect is a foundation of education irrespective of race, religion, disability, sexual identity or gender identity. It is the philosophy of inclusion. The need for appropriate RSE is paramount.

KEY POINTS

- Same-sex relationships have been recorded for the past 10,000 years, through the accepted timeline of civilisation.
- Transgender identity has been recorded for nearly 9,000 years.
- Evidence for same-sex relationships and transgender identity have been found globally.
- It is difficult for us to understand different cultures at different times due to our 21st-century perspective in our own culture.
- There has been an undulating criminalisation of same-sex relationships where what was once legal had been criminalised and vice versa.

(Continued)

- Numerous individuals have sought to extend the discussion on the acceptance of gender identity and same-sex relationships.
- Various individuals have been killed for their gender and/or sexual identity.
- Bias incidents and hate crimes are prevalent in our society today.
- A history of advocacy has developed, initially via protests, although also through education.

LESSONS IN LOVE & UNDERSTANDING 5: GENDER AND SEXOLOGY THROUGH THE AGES

(For the RSE teaching that we advocate, 4-year-olds can be included in the KS1 learning and 17-year-olds can be included in the KS4 learning.)

KS1 (AGE 5–7 YEARS)

- Create a rainbow and ask pupils to draw pictures of things they personally find important in their lives and/or that they identify with in some way. Explain the importance of everybody's pictures being represented, even when other people have the same ideas or very different ideas – everybody has their ideas included on the rainbow. Talk about the rainbow symbol and the different things it symbolises. Ask the class what rainbows make them think of, or feel like.
- Explain the concept of positive role models and ask children to draw or make a collage of their role model/superhero. Explain that this is to be a person or thing that they admire for their behaviour and the loving traits that they show. They can write words around their picture to describe the amazing things about their super hero.
- Refer to a child-friendly poster on the UN Convention of the Rights of a Child and run an empowerment session, asking pupils to form children's rules lists that reflect their rights.
- Share appropriate literature as suggested in our recommended reading.

KS2 (AGE 7–11 YEARS)

- Discuss what everyday behaviours should be outlawed. For example, should students be banned from using an electronic device for more than an hour during the weekend. Discuss how they would feel, how they would get around this, and their thoughts on unfair punishments.

- Look at a child-friendly version of the Universal Rights of the Child (links provided in the Additional resources at the end of Chapter 8), and ask the class to choose one of the rights to discuss in pairs/groups and create a poster to represent this and feed back to the class.

- Ask pupils to write a letter to the headteacher, expressing what they think their class needs to learn in RSE. Give helpful cues such as 'what I need to learn about relationships', 'what kind of things I need to know about the human developing body', 'what I need to know about sex and how babies are made', 'what I need my family/ guardians to know', and so on.

- Share appropriate literature, as suggested in the Additional reading below.

KS3 (AGE 11–14 YEARS)

- Encourage the students to make a time capsule of ten items that portray males and females in the 21st century. Then encourage the students to consider a gender-neutral time capsule.

- Develop a poster demonstrating the level of hate crime experienced in relation to LGBTQI+, disability, race or religion. Mathematical skills such as constructing pie charts could be used, combined with design skills such as Microsoft Publisher or PowerPoint.

- Choose an item the student has easy access to – for example, their pencil case, a pen, etc. Encourage them to think about what it would be like if they were discriminated against for having the wrong type of pen or the wrong logo on their pencil case. From this, encourage the students to write a letter to an agony aunt/uncle about an aspect they have been discriminated against. Extend this further by getting the students to swap letters and to write a reply.

- Invite the students to research and present the biography of a famous LGBTQI+ icon such as Freddie Mercury, Judy Garland, Miley Cyrus, Oscar Wilde, Caitlyn Jenner, Indya Moore, etc.

KS4 (AGE 14–16 YEARS)

- Encourage the students to articulate a debate about LGBTQI+ laws – for example, holding a retrial of Oscar Wilde today. This could be

(Continued)

supported by encouraging the students to write newspaper reports on the trial.

- Investigate the history of protest. Why do people protest? How effective are they? Parallels could be made with the past and present – for example, the recent protests in Hong Kong through to more historic protests. News footage of Section 28 can be found on the internet which could lead to a debate about Section 28.
- Challenge students to consider how they would act as advocates in their own or other people's fights against injustice. Theme this more specifically to RSE, perhaps providing some scenarios for the students to choose to represent.
- Develop an infographic using freely available software (such as Piktochart) to portray historical or current debates, or alternatively information concerning hate crimes. From this, the students could establish three principles to help address such hate crimes.

ADDITIONAL READING

KS1 (AGE 5–7 YEARS)

- *We Are All Born Free: The Universal Declaration of Human Rights in Pictures* by Amnesty International.
- *There's a Bear on My Chair* by Ross Collins.
- *My Little Book of Big Freedoms* by Chris Riddell.
- *A is for Activist* by Innosanto Nagara.

KS2 (AGE 7–11 YEARS)

- *Children Who Changed The World: Incredible True Stories About Children's Rights!* by Marcia Williams.
- *The Boy at the Back of the Class* by Onjali Rauf.
- *The Truth Pixie Goes to School* by Matt Haig.
- *Usborne Politics for Beginners* by Louie Stowell, Alex Frith, Rosie Hore and Kellan Stover.
- *Real Friends* by Shannon Hale and LeUyen Pham.

KS3 (AGE 11–14 YEARS)

- *The Poet X* by Elizabeth Acevedo.
- *Stargirl* by Jerry Spinelli.

- *Story of a Girl* by Sara Zarr.
- *Girl Rising: Changing the World One Girl at a Time* by Tanya Lee Stone.
- *Every Day* by David Levithan.
- *The Miseducation of Cameron Post* by Emily M. Danforth.

KS4 (AGE 14–16 YEARS)

- *LGBT: The Survival Guide for Lesbian, Gay, Bisexual, Transgender, and Questioning Teens* by Kelly Huegel Madrone.
- *It Gets Better: Coming Out, Overcoming Bully, and Creating a Life Worth Living* by Dan Savage and Terry Miller.
- *Fight Like a Girl: 50 Feminists Who Changed the World* by Laura Barcella.
- *Queer, There, and Everywhere: 23 People Who Changed the World* by Sarah Prager.
- *How We Fight for our Lives: A Memoir* by Saeed Jones.
- *How to Cure a Ghost* by Fariha Róisín and Monica Ramos.
- *Living Proof: Telling Your Story to Make a Difference* by John Capecci and Timothy Cage.
- *Modern HERstory: Stories of Women and Ordinary People Rewriting History* by Blair Imani.
- *Stung with Love: Poems and Fragments of Sappho* by Sappho.

ADULTS

- *From Prejudice to Pride: A History of LGBTQ+ Movement* by Amy Lamé.
- *Pride: The Story of the LGBTQ Equality Movement* by Matthew Todd.
- *We Are Everywhere: Protest, Power, and Pride in the History of Queer Liberation* by Matthew Riemer and Leighton Brown.
- *Boy Erased: A Memoir of Identity, Faith, and Family* by Garrard Conley.

6

POLICY, GUIDANCE AND SIGNPOSTING FOR TEACHERS

CONTENTS

CHAPTER OBJECTIVES

- To understand what the RSE 2020 policy is and why it has been developed.
- To appreciate a range of implications for developing a school's RSE policy.
- To consider the relevant content and coverage for different key stages and age groups.
- To understand what is required of a school policy on RSE.
- To understand the legal requirements for RSE 2020.

WHY THIS CHAPTER?

Please be honest. When was the last time you consulted your school's policy on inclusion, or indeed, any other policy for that matter? You may know where to find the policies; however, do you tend to just follow the same procedures as everybody else? Consider the policy that you may not have read in greater detail. Why was it written? What purpose does it serve? Who wrote it and when? Have you questioned the policy? Or perhaps you just do what is expected.

The next three chapters will take a slightly different format, as we are going to help you look at the 2020 policy and show you how to apply this in a meaningful way, within your teaching and your school. In order to do this, we would like to break down the policy and give some clear examples of how this might look in real terms in your professional world. All of this, of course, applies to the Lessons in Chapters 1–5, but these chapters are also transferable as general HR guidance, which could be applied to any public setting or workplace.

Education is ever changing, ever transforming, as are we as teachers and as are our students. Just as Heraclitus asserted that you cannot step in the same river twice, the flow of education continues to evolve for a variety of reasons. Like a river, some policies are slow-moving, requiring little change from year to year. Yet a rainstorm can bring fundamental changes up-river so that the water becomes fast and swift-flowing. So – RSE 2020: a passing shower or a torrential downpour?

How we respond to this question depends on our perspective. Education is not a series of right practices: instead, it is a series of informed practices that we continually refine, depending on who we are and who we work with at a certain moment in time. If it was just a series of 'right' practices, there would be only one book on how to teach and ultimately teachers could be replaced by robots. Education is far more nuanced.

This chapter therefore considers how we can take and work with RSE 2020, striving to implement it in our unique educational setting. Please note that some of the terminology cited in this chapter comes directly from policy – for example, the Science National Curriculum – and, as such, may appear somewhat dated in relation to current parlance on RSE.

RSE 2020 AS IT STANDS

The Government do not just click their fingers and conjure up a policy, although it may sometimes feel like this is what they are doing. If we return to the river metaphor used earlier, there are many tributaries that inform Government policy, all feeding into a river with a collective force. RSE 2020 was no different. Groups such as Mumsnet and the PTA UK, along with YouGov polls about the risks of sexting, the need for online safety given the associated risks of growing up in an increasingly digital world, and teaching unions calling for statutory status indicated that parents and schools wanted universal coverage for all pupils and improved quality in relation to relationships education in the modern world.

The final statutory guidance was informed by 23,000 responses from parents, young people, schools and experts, with a subsequent public consultation where 40,000 people replied. The statutory guidance concerns issues under Section 80A of the Education Act 2002 and Section 403 of the Education Act 1996. Consequently, the public have had a say on how RSE 2020 is shaped. Furthermore, while 'statutory guidance' may be perceived as just that, guidance, within the education context, statutory guidance establishes what schools and local authorities must do to comply with the law. Although we have referred to the document as 'RSE 2020' throughout this book, it saves us repeating the full title of the 'Statutory guidance: Relationships education, relationships and sex education (RSE) and health education' (DfE, 2019).

While the statutory guidance predominantly focuses on RSE, the health education component is less contentious, and the guidance is more specific in nature. Consequently, this book has focused on RSE while implicitly incorporating references to health education (such as mental health and well-being) throughout.

THE POLICY

The policy statement that initiated RSE 2020 specified that 'we do not think it is right to specify the exact content of subjects as this would be too prescriptive, removing freedom from schools and running the risk of the legislation becoming quickly out of date as the world changes' (DfE, 2017). From this, the policy extended to explain that all primary schools would be required to provide relationships education while being able to choose to teach age-appropriate sex education. Secondary schools would be required to cover relationships and sex education. Furthermore, the policy explained that the themes and issues (which should be covered in an age-appropriate way) would likely focus on:

- Different types of relationship. In primary schools this would cover aspects such as friendships, family relationships and dealing with strangers. At secondary, this would be extended to intimate relationships.
- How to recognise, understand and build healthy relationships. This would cover self-respect, respect for others, commitment and tolerance, boundaries and consent, dealing with conflict and recognising unhealthy relationships.
- The effect of relationships on health and well-being, including mental health.
- Healthy relationships and staying safe online.
- Secondary schools would be required to provide factual knowledge around sex, sexual health and sexuality within the context of relationships. (While the RSE 2020 policy frames the teaching of

sex, sexual health and sexuality within the context of relationships, as authors we would challenge the policy. As we have discussed in Chapters 4 and 5, students may be involved in sexual activity for a range of reasons and we would urge the policy writers to consider this when the policy is revised.)

REQUIREMENTS FOR ALL SCHOOLS

Pupil referral units, alternative provision academies, free schools and independent schools are required to make provision for RSE education in the same way as mainstream schools, with specific thought given to the needs and vulnerabilities of students. There is no specific guidance for children who are home schooled within the policy. However, we feel that this is an important area for inclusion in any curriculum for home-schooled children.

SENSITIVITY

RSE 2020 discusses how, when teaching about families, there needs to be a degree of sensitivity due to different family structures – specifically, that there is no stigmatisation of children based on their home circumstances. For example, a student may be located in one of a multitude of family structures, for a range of reasons, including one-, two- or more parent families, and so forth. Families might have any number of private or social issues affecting them that school has no way of knowing about, around relationships, identity, health and well-being. Jude shares specific sex education teaching experience at mainstream schools:

> I'm trained in providing community education, and in my role I visit many schools at Key Stages 2, 3 and 4 to provide RSE. What I need to know about the pupils I am going to be working with is their level of understanding and the way in which I can make the content of what I deliver accessible to all. So quite often I am setting up with classroom and SEN assistants to ensure the sessions are appropriate and work well for everybody. I am well aware that there will be kids in any group who are affected by domestic violence, loss, and any number of challenges in their family or home lives. It's important I am always sensitive to this and that I encourage the group to be

thoughtful and considerate since we don't know what anybody else's home life is like. (Jude, age 25)

In addition, there may be child protection concerns to be aware of. For example, as the student enters secondary education and there is greater discussion on abusive relationships, there may be a specific student who has or is experiencing such a relationship that you are unaware of. To this extent, ensure that you have a discussion with your Designated Safeguarding Lead (DSL) about any content you intend to cover and when, and also whether this may affect any at-risk students. This provides an opportunity for the DSL to consider the appropriate way forward.

> **Tip 1** In all social education, begin the lesson by explaining that there may be some issues that might feel sensitive to some people in the group, as they touch on issues that are or have been affecting them in their real lives at home, or that they may experience in the future. Ask the group or class to be kind, caring and sensitive in what they say or do with an awareness that we never know what is going on for somebody else at any time. This is a great lesson in compassion, empathy and helping students of all ages see that everybody is different. Empathy can be taught.

> **Tip 2** As a teacher, always teach the class making the assumption that there are pupils under your care who are vulnerable and at risk and/or dealing with the issues that you discuss in their home lives. This way you are always mindful of delivering from a fair and loving place, and you provide the opportunity for students to talk to you, should they wish. At the beginning of the lesson you might offer students a way of having a conversation with you about anything that has affected them within the lesson – for example, some classes have a sign-up list for a slot to talk one-to-one with the teacher, and this is scheduled. For older students, it might be possible that they can email to arrange a meeting.

PARENTAL RIGHT TO WITHDRAW

The latest policy explains that parents maintain a right to withdraw their child from sex education within RSE. However, they would not be able to withdraw their child from relationships education in primary school, nor would they be able to withdraw their child from sex education as part of the National Curriculum for Science.

If a parent chooses to withdraw their child from the sex education component, it is important for schools to keep a record of any communication, such as any email or telephone requests, or ideally a dated letter. RSE 2020 highlights that it is good practice for the school to discuss the importance of sex education and any detrimental effects that withdrawal may have on the student. For example, the social and emotional effects of being excluded, the likelihood that the student will hear their peers' interpretation of what was covered in the lessons, and so forth. However, a parent can only request the right to withdraw their child up to and until three terms before their child turns 16, after which, the student can make their own decision.

AGE-APPROPRIATE CONTENT

Within the policy, it was stated that relationships education and RSE would be required to be appropriate to the age of the pupils, and that the Secretary of State must provide guidance to schools on how to deliver this. However, at the time of writing, no such guidance has been issued.

> **Tip 3** Age is not an accurate indicator of appropriateness, as we know human development and experience is diverse and varied. The main consideration as a teacher and parent is safety and child protection. There are certain things that children and young people have a right to know and learn in order to make safe choices and protect them from harm. This must be taken very seriously if a parent chooses to withdraw a child from lessons that provide vital social education and life skills.

SEND

The policy outlines that students deemed to have SEND are more vulnerable to exploitation, bullying and other issues in relation to RSE. Therefore, we must ensure that any educational content is developed at an applicable level for SEND students to access, specifically given the different developmental stages of students.

Tip 4 Of course, SEND should be taken into consideration as they would be with any other lesson in making the learning appropriate for each student.

RELIGIOUS BACKGROUND

In relation to religious background, the policy statement specified that relationship education and RSE would need to have provision to be appropriate to the religious background of pupils, specifically enabling faith schools to teach relationships and sex education according to the tenets of their faith, while still being consistent with the requirements of the Equality Act 2010. This is covered under paragraph 27 of the statutory guidance. As we have discussed throughout this book, there are most probably people from every country and culture who identify as LGBTQI+, while some people belonging to factions of various religious and faith groups believe inclusion of LGBTQI+ in RSE teaching to be against the discipline of their faith. Our core assertion throughout this book is that of respect for the individual, including that their sense of self must be protected within the requirements of British law. This means that it is as unfair for RSE to exclude people belonging to LGBTQI+ communities as it would be to exclude anyone based on religious or cultural background – for example, it would be prejudiced to refuse to recognise a legal marriage as legitimate because it belonged to a certain faith community or people of an LGBTQI+ community.

Tip 5 As a reminder, the protected characteristics of the Equality Act are age, disability, gender reassignment, marriage and civil partnership, pregnancy and maternity, race, religion or belief, sex, and sexual orientation. Furthermore, under paragraph 28 of the statutory guidance, schools must not unlawfully discriminate against pupils in relation to the protected characteristics of the Equality Act.

Although the policy statement does not contain reference to British values, it has been a requirement that they are promoted by all schools since 2014. Values consist of: democracy, the rule of law, individual liberty, and mutual respect and tolerance of those with different faiths and beliefs.

(Continued)

Consequently, faith schools would need to ensure that there is coverage of the full spectrum of society: heterosexual, disability, LGBTQI+, other religions – all of which cannot be discriminated against even if this is at odds with the teachings, and their interpretation of the teachings, of their faith, otherwise there would be a breach of the Equality Act and requirement to respect British values.

Specifically, in the introduction to the statutory guidance, it is suggested that 'schools with a religious character may teach the distinctive faith perspective on relationships, and balanced debate may take place about issues that are seen as contentious'. The introduction progresses to explain that 'the school may wish to reflect on faith teachings about certain topics as well as how their faith institutions may support people in matters of relationships and sex'. An example that resonates with the themes in this book is the perennial philosophy (or universal tradition across all world religions) of love.

Ali teaches at a secondary school with a high proportion of Muslim pupils.

I must admit that RSE is not my favourite part of the syllabus. I'm the RSE lead at my school, though, and it's been a better experience so far than I expected. Some parents and family members of our students do have a lot of fears around what we might teach, so our communication with them around this is key. When it is explained that actually their kids need to know about this stuff to keep them safe, and so they can make informed decisions, people tend to relax a lot. At the end of the day we are here to teach good values, and equality and diversity have to be a part of that. (Ali, age 30)

Tip 6 Schools with a religious character absolutely can teach the perspective of the particular faith they belong to on relationships . . . but this must be balanced alongside other perspectives, remembering too that people belonging to the same religion more often than not have differing views and perspectives about individual identity within their shared faith group. Healthy education means that teachers can safely facilitate structured debate on any contentious issue, which will not only allow a far greater depth of understanding into the differing views and beliefs of others, but also teaches that there is room for us all on this planet, and we can share our thoughts and ideas without it meaning war.

LGBT

In a letter from Damian Hinds, the then Secretary of State for Education, to Paul Whiteman, the General Secretary of the National Association for Head Teachers, on 9 April 2019, Mr Hinds explained that LGBT relationship education needs to be covered during a student's school years, with an expectation that this is covered in secondary schools. Consequently, we would like to direct you to Chapter 2 for further guidance.

> **Tip 7** In relation to the RSE 2020 policy, age-appropriate teaching relates to the S part of RSE and not LGBT content. As discussed in Chapter 3, relationships include an array of families and family structures that need to be taught at primary level; consequently, it is necessary to include LGBTQI+ families. Chapters 2 and 3 provide specific guidance for including this at Key Stage 1 and 2 if you are not already doing so.

PRIMARY FOCUS

Within the primary phase, relationships education should focus on the foundation blocks and characteristics for developing positive relationships – specifically friendships, family relationships, relationships with other children and relationships with other adults. Although primary schools do not have to teach sex education, the policy states in paragraph 66 that all primary schools should teach about puberty as part of the National Curriculum for Science in which the development of the human body from birth to old age (including puberty) needs to be covered, along with reproduction in some plants and animals. As authors, we would advise you to proceed with caution and sensitivity when using traditional scientific resources to explain human development and reproduction. To describe human life as a collection of cells and roll dice to look at genetics and 'how we were made' simply fails to see the person as a thinking being with a heart, mind and soul. It is not helpful in learning about relationships and real families or in building self-esteem. You can find alternative resources at: www.lessonsinlove.info.

More information can be found in the statutory guidance, paragraphs 54–68, and we have provided further guidance under Lessons in Love & Understanding 3.

Tip 8 The teaching around puberty and human development plus reproduction is rather outdated when taught with a scientific approach. After all, babies and children come to belong in families in all kinds of ways, and not everybody is able or desires to have sex or reproduce. The other interesting thing about how we teach human development at schools is that we appear to hit puberty, everybody panics, we rush our way through relationships and sex, and forget the rest. Nobody ever teaches about the menopause and andropause, and what happens as we become elderly. Nobody ever teaches about when our bodies aren't developing as we expected or there are differences, disability or illness. It becomes apparent that there are huge cross-sections of society that we omit when teaching about RSE. We seem to promote some kind of superior model of being and reproducing based on the healthiest, strongest and most fertile of the species. This does not reflect reality and we seem to be endorsing a rather authoritarian way of viewing the world. RSE should be meaningful in a way that students (and teachers) can reflect on their real lives, and the real world and real people around them.

SECONDARY FOCUS

For the secondary phase, relationship and sex education should focus on extending the primary phase, continuing to develop healthy, nurturing relationships, specifically what a healthy relationship might look like, such as what makes a good friend or other type of committed relationships. A core understanding is the way in which good relationships can be beneficial to mental well-being and how to manage relationships that are not conducive to mental and emotional well-being. In relation to intimate relationships, the focus is on developing such relationships, resisting the pressure to have sex, along with not applying pressure, plus **safer sex** and contraception. Further information can be found in the statutory guidance, paragraphs 69–82, and we have provided some guidance under Lessons in Love & Understanding 3.

RSE EXPECTATIONS WITHIN OTHER SUBJECTS

Within the national curriculum, there are several subjects that lend themselves to covering aspects of RSE 2020. The following subjects contain specific content that is expected to be taught as part of RSE.

- National curriculum for science (Key Stages 1 and 2). The main external parts of the body, and changes to the body as it grows from birth to old age, including puberty.
- National curriculum for citizenship (Key Stages 3 and 4). Develop awareness and understanding of democracy, government, how laws are developed, how laws are upheld, making reasoned arguments based on reputable evidence.
- National curriculum for science (Key Stages 3 and 4). Reproduction in humans – e.g. the structure and function of the reproductive systems for males and females, the menstrual cycle, gametes, fertilisation, gestation, birth, HIV and AIDS.
- National curriculum for computing. Age-progressive e-safety.

INCLUSION

One aspect overlooked by the policy is that of inclusion. Inclusion is more than a series of bullet points or a checklist: it is a shared philosophy that goes beyond any boundaries. It is more than acceptance, more than making provision for others; it permeates everything within a school community. Because relationships and sex education may feel threatening, or perhaps more accurately, fear-invoking to some, as both a school and as a wider society, honest, open discussion will help resolve tensions. This is why the RSE 2020 policy asserts that any school policy needs to be discussed with the full school community.

DEVELOPING A POLICY: PRESCRIBED CONTENT

You may have developed numerous policies previously or this could be your first one. Either way, being tasked with developing what has been perceived as a contentious policy can be daunting. If this has been delegated to you, it means that someone knows that you can do a stunning job and they have not just passed it your way to avoid the responsibility. Well done. The following guidance should help.

The statutory guidance requires that all schools write a school policy for RSE, a policy that must include parental consultation in its development and review. As previously noted, the policy must reflect the community that the school serves in order to meet the needs of the students and the parents, and must be included on the school's website and made freely available to anyone who requests it.

Within both the primary and secondary sector, the basic policy needs to:

- Define what is meant by relationships education (for primary) and relationships and sex education (for secondary).
  - As RSE 2020 does not actually define what RSE is, an agreed definition needs to be established for your policy. We have provided a definition here that could be used as a basis based on wording from the Policy Statement (2017), RSE 2020, and Briefing Paper Number 06103, authored by Long (2019).
  - Primary: Relationship and Sex Education (RSE) is a compulsory part of the school curriculum. Relationship education focuses on the ability to recognise, understand, form and develop different types of healthy relationships such as friendships, family relationships, dealing with strangers, and so forth. Sex education is the factual knowledge around human body parts and reproduction. (Note that at the end of this sentence, you may choose to add: sex education within primary schools is not compulsory, therefore we will only focus on relationships education and the coverage of puberty as required in the national curriculum for science.)
  - Secondary: Relationship and Sex Education (RSE) is a compulsory part of the school curriculum. Relationship education focuses on the ability to recognise, understand, form and develop different types of healthy relationships such as friendships, family relationships, dealing with strangers, and intimate relationships. Sex education is the factual knowledge around sex, sexual health and sexuality, which is firmly established within the context of relationships.
- Outline the subject content, including how it is taught and who is responsible for the teaching of it.
  - Primary: the subject content consists of families and people who care for me, caring friendships, respectful relationships, online relationships and being safe. Specific details are included in Appendix A. (Here, we would suggest that you include the table under paragraph 62 of RSE 2020, pages 20–2.)
  - Secondary: the subject content consists of families; respectful relationships, including friendships; online and media; being

safe; intimate sexual relationships, including sexual health. Specific details are included in Appendix A. (Here, we would suggest that you include the table under paragraph 81 of RSE 2020, pages 27–9.)

- o Relationship (and sex) education lessons will be taught by the class teacher (or detail the role of the person who will be teaching this, such as the form teacher, PSHE lead, deputy headteacher) and they will be responsible to the RSE policy committee.

- Include the monitoring and evaluation of the subject.
  - o The RSE policy committee will be responsible for the monitoring and evaluation of RSE, through the standard monitoring and evaluation approach adopted for all subjects. (Note: your school may have a policy in place for monitoring and evaluation which you can refer to.)

- Clarify why parents do not have a right to withdraw their child from the subject (for primary relationships education) or clarify the parent's right to request that their child is withdrawn from the sex education component within RSE.
  - o Primary: by law, all children need to participate in relationships education and parents cannot request their child's withdrawal. Additionally, children are not allowed to be withdrawn from the national curriculum science component, which covers the development of the human body from birth to old age (including puberty), along with reproduction in some plants and animals. Parents can, however, request that their child is withdrawn from any additional teaching in relation to sex education.
  - o Secondary: by law, all children need to participate in relationships education and parents cannot request their child's withdrawal. Additionally, children are not allowed to be withdrawn from the national curriculum science component which covers reproduction in humans – for example, the structure and function of the human reproductive systems, menstrual cycle, gametes, fertilisation, gestation, birth and HIV/AIDS. Parents can, however, request that their child is withdrawn from any additional teaching in relation to sex education up to and until three terms before their child turns 16. After this time, the student can decide on whether they would like to be taught sex education. If they do decide to be

taught the sex education component, the school will ensure that appropriate provision is made.
- Provide a date when the policy will be reviewed.
  - The policy will be reviewed every three years, or whenever the policy or curriculum for RSE changes.

In addition, the policy may include the following sections:

- A header, including the policy title, when it is effective from and the revision date.
- An introduction to the policy, outlining what the policy concerns and why it is required.
- Definitions: it is worth providing a list of acronyms at the start of the policy and then defining terms as the policy progresses. It may also be worth including a glossary at the end of the document.
- The scheme of work and the content of each topic, highlighting the relevant age when this will be covered.
  - Please refer to Lessons in Love & Understanding 3 for guidance.
- The person responsible for teaching relationships education, or relationships and sex education.
- The procedures in which the policy has been developed and how it will be reviewed.
  - It is important to note that the policy needs to be developed as a collaborative process with students, parents, governors, teachers and other stakeholders.
  - Suggestions for such collaboration involve convening a governors meeting to outline the new requirements, what is required, why the policy needs to be changed, and so forth. A working party can then be established to write and review the policy, then monitor that the policy is being embedded.
  - A further suggestion is to hold a parental consultation evening where staff and governors can discuss the new policy and how the school has taken responsibility for shaping it in accordance with core guidance and the law.
  - A suggestion box, generic e-mail address (e.g. info@school name.sch.uk) or online form could be established to enable parents to provide suggestions or comments on the new policy.

- How the content will be made accessible to all pupils, including those with SEND.
  - Discuss how the content will be differentiated.
- Outline the procedures for how the parent may withdraw their child from the sex education component.
  - You may include, for example, that parents may request that their child is withdrawn from the sex education component. A request will need to be made in writing, specifying their child's name and including the date the request has been made. You will be invited to discuss your concerns about the sex education component with the school, and this in turn will be recorded regarding the date of any meeting or whether this invitation has been declined.
- The requirements for schools to teach RSE in relation to the law, along with the appropriate guidance that has informed the policy. At a minimum, you should include the following:
  - There is a legal requirement to teach RSE as outlined in the following documents:
  - Department for Education (2017) policy statement: relationships education, relationships and sex education, and personal, social, health and economic education. Available at: https://assets.publishing.service.gov.uk/government/uploads/attachment_data/file/595828/170301_Policy_statement_PSHEv2.pdf
  - Department for Education (2019) statutory guidance: relationships education, relationships and sex education (RSE) and health education. Available at: www.gov.uk/government/publications/relationships-education-relationships-and-sex-education-rse-and-health-education
  - Legislation.gov.uk (2010) Equality Act 2010. Available at: www.legislation.gov.uk/ukpga/2010/15/contents
  - Legislation.gov.uk (2014) The Education (Independent School Standards) (England) (Amendment) Regulations 2014 (Number 2374). (This is more commonly known as 'British Values'.) Available at: www.legislation.gov.uk/uksi/2014/2374/pdfs/uksi_20142374_en.pdf
- The frequency with which the policy will be updated.
- The person or people responsible for approving the policy.

CONCLUSION

The previous chapters have provided a background to RSE that we hope has been read before starting work on developing a school policy. A range of themes inherent within RSE 2020 have been outlined and simplified to provide a pragmatic overview of what schools must do and why, with guidance for developing school policy.

KEY POINTS

- RSE 2020 has been developed over a two-year time frame, instigated through the changing nature of society including the online world, along with calls from various interest groups. It has included the voices of parents, young people, schools and experts, with a subsequent wider public consultation.
- There is a legal requirement to teach RSE in primary and secondary schools.
- RSE always needs to be facilitated sensitively regardless of the student group, as we may never know anyone's background. Ensure that you speak to your DSL about any content you intend to cover in case there are at-risk students, where certain topics may cause specific distress.
- RSE needs to be age appropriate and to take account of students' needs and abilities (e.g. SEND).
- RSE does have cross-curricular links, predominantly with the national curriculum for science and computing.
- Parents can request that their child is withdrawn from the sex education component of RSE. However, they cannot request that their child is withdrawn from sex education within the science curriculum: at primary, this includes puberty and at secondary it is reproduction in humans.
- Under the 2010 Equality Act and British Values, gender orientation and/or sexual identity cannot be discriminated against, in the same way that other protected characteristics cannot similarly be discriminated against, such as disability, race, religion or belief.
- There must be inclusion of LGBT. For example, highlighting that irrespective of how a person identifies in gender or sexual orientation, they cannot be discriminated against, even if this is at odds with a student's or teacher's religious or cultural background.

Factual information must be presented with a balanced debate, while consideration of how to support individuals from a religious or belief perspective can be included.
- All schools are required to develop a policy in consultation with a range of stakeholders.

TEACHING RESOURCES

There are many excellent free resources available for schools to use when teaching these subjects. Schools should carefully assess each resource they propose to use to ensure they are appropriate for the age and maturity of pupils and sensitive to their needs. Where relevant, schools should use resources that are medically accurate. Schools should also consider the expertise of the main subject associations who often quality assure third-party resources.

We also recognise that schools use resources from representative bodies – for example, many Catholic and other schools use the model curricula provided by the Catholic Education Service. Other representative bodies should be consulted to reflect the needs of your students.

Schools should also ensure that when they consult parents, they provide examples of the resources they plan to use. This can be reassuring for parents and enables them to continue the conversations started in class at home.

We would also like to reiterate the need to ensure that any safe searching for RSE content adheres to your school's policy, especially if you have a work laptop that you may be using. It would be easy for your search history to raise a number of 'red flags' on the school system, where you have been searching for content for RSE lessons. It would be worth speaking to your DSL, information/technology manager and headteacher about this.

ADDITIONAL RESOURCES

The list below is for illustrative purposes and is not exhaustive.

- For safeguarding, the NSPCC 'PANTS' resources for schools and teachers may be found at: https://learning.nspcc.org.uk/research-resources/schools/pants-teaching/

- An example model primary school curriculum from the Catholic Education Service may be found at: http://catholiceducation.org.uk/schools/relationship-sex-education
- For current information on all aspects of sexual and reproductive health, the following website is useful: www.sexwise.fpa.org.uk/
- The following website from the PSHE Association provides useful resources for 'Disrespect NoBody' teaching: www.pshe-association.org.uk/curriculum-and-resources/resources/disrespect-nobody-teaching-resources-preventing
- The PSHE Association also provide guidance for teaching about consent: www.pshe-association.org.uk/curriculum-and-resources/resources/guidance-teaching-about-consent-pshe-education-key
- For LGBT inclusivity, the resources from Stonewall for both primary and secondary are extremely useful: www.stonewall.org.uk/resources/different-families-same-love-pack
- The Public Health England website 'Rise Above for Schools' provides a range of resources covering relationships and bullying, alcohol, smoking, stress, and body image, with videos made by young people and resources tested with teachers: https://campaignresources.phe.gov.uk/schools/topics/rise-above/overview?WT.mc_id=RiseAboveforSchools_PSHEA_EdComs_Resource_listing_Sep17
- In relation to mental well-being, a free education resource is available from MindEd: www.minded.org.uk
- Further mental well-being resources are available from the PSHE Association: www.pshe-association.org.uk/curriculum-and-resources/resources/guidance-teaching-about-mental-health-and
- For online safety, the following Government publication provides useful information: www.gov.uk/government/publications/education-for-a-connected-world
- For safe internet use, resources to education about sexting, and so forth, the UK Council for Internet Safety is located at: www.gov.uk/government/organisations/uk-council-for-internet-safety
- The education programme from the National Crime Agency (NCA)–Child Exploitation Online Programme (CEOP), provides guidance to protect children both online and offline. The site offers materials for parents, teachers and pupils on a wide range of online safety issues and facts about areas such as digital footprints, recognising fake websites and checking URLs. It is available at: www.thinkuknow.co.uk/

- For more general PSHE content, refer to: www.pshe-association. org.uk/curriculum-and-resources/resources/programme-study-pshe-education-key-stages-1–5
- Although beyond the scope of this book, information for planning effective drugs and alcohol education may be found at: http:// mentor-adepis.org/planning-effective-education/
- For information relating to extremism and radicalisation, 'Educate Against Hate' provides practical advice and information for teachers: https://educateagainsthate.com
- Guidance on Citizenship education may be found at: www.gov.uk/ government/publications/citizenship-programmes-of-study-for-key-stages-1-and-2
- Data is available from Public Health England to help understand the health and well-being needs of the local school-age population, including health profiles for school-age children and young people. The indicators allow areas to see how they perform against the national average and against other local areas. This may be found at: https://fingertips.phe.org.uk/profile/child-health-profiles
- The Public Health websites for other countries are listed below, although current health profiles are yet to be published.
  - Ireland: www.publichealth.ie/
  - Scotland: https://consult.gov.scot/public-health/public-health-scotland/
  - Wales: https://phw.nhs.wales/

7

ESTABLISHING A SAFE LEARNING AND TEACHING SPACE

CONTENTS

> ## CHAPTER OBJECTIVES
>
> - To understand how a supportive context can be provided for teaching RSE.
> - To comprehend the seven steps for planning and running RSE teaching blocks.
> - To appreciate how various common scenarios may be approached.

WHY THIS CHAPTER?

In Chapter 6 we have taken a close look at Government policy and guidelines for schools in England and how that looks in real-life education. In this chapter we are going to guide you through our safe steps to running RSE, creating a space conducive to relaxed learning, which promotes health and well-being for all. Again, our structure for this chapter is designed to illustrate the step-by-step nature of our approach.

Good teachers are many things to many people, and mainstream education often positions the good teacher in extra roles including social worker, IT expert, detective, nurse, nutritionist, physical trainer, chef, interior designer, actor . . . we could go on. What we do not want to do in this book is add to those roles in making you sexologist, agony aunt, relationship counsellor and endocrinologist. Our intention is to pull RSE into line with everything else you are already doing in terms of quality and provision.

Let's recap on *Lessons in Love & Understanding* so far. We have asked that you take both a personally and professionally reflective journey of discovery looking at constructs of self, gender, relationships, sexuality and sex. We have looked at history, geography, politics, religion, philosophy, media, biology, chemistry and psychology. In fact, we have covered most of the subjects you teach. You are a pro with this stuff, you are a great teacher – we know this as you have the motivation to be reading this book. We hope to have torn down the false walls of social constructs and rickety scaffolding of ideas that humans and society have erected in an attempt to mask our colourful real lives within a concrete façade of drab uniformity. Now it's time to start from scratch, from the inner core, and lay a solid, true foundation to build the Taj Mahal of RSE.

CREATING LOVING SPACES

Many of the things we can do to make the world a better place won't break the school budget. They simply require thoughtfulness. As we have suggested throughout the book, it is about using inclusive language and being as conscious as possible not to make assumptions about gender and sexuality when working with any kind of social scenario, be it fictional or real life, in your place of education, and to represent all styles of family life and break free of the heteronormative narrative that can be so stifling to so many people.

Remember this applies to staff, too. Let's not forget the teachers. All too often our emphasis is on children and families, and we forget about looking after the educator. In this chapter, we hope to explain just how important your self-care, peer support and supervision are in maintaining your own health and well-being, and ensuring you too are nurtured in the workplace and the process of your own educational CPD. As we know, the modelling of behaviours has a profound impact on learning, so here we have three reasons why your staff team should demonstrate equal opportunity and inclusion not just as policy, but reflected in the place of education, throughout the hierarchy, in a whole-school approach.

Resources need not cost any more than your school already budgets for. Again, it is about choosing literature and media that reflect a wide range of people and families. Please note that we are not just talking about LGBTQI+ representation. We need to be seeing families with disability, with mental health issues, and mixed-race families, blended families, single parent families, foster families – we are all out there, so let's be seen and heard. We must be very conscious of our wall displays, of the materials we provide and, if the resources do not reflect society, let's take that to the class. It can be a simple question or statement observing how a picture might look different from many other 'normal' families. It's about raising awareness that actually very few children tick every box of being white, middle class, living with 1.4 other siblings, none with special needs or other birth parents, and a happily married Christian heterosexual binary cisgender female mum and male dad. We don't have the true statistics, but how many families do you know that tick all those boxes? (See Chapter 4 for more on this.) We can't all be 'abnormal'.

Practical facilities, like those stated before in Chapter 2, are also normally simple. There is no need for gender-specific toilets. You could create new unisex signs in one of your lessons. Dressing for sports can either be done discretely in the classroom, dressing rooms or kids can dress privately in toilet cubicles where there is no provision of unisex changing cubicles. Times are changing, and most public sports facilities have unisex changing cubicles. Again, it's not just the LGBTQI+ communities that benefit from this. There are numerous reasons that many people do not want to dress or undress in public view. Everybody has a right to privacy.

Names are the other simple one. In many schools and places of education, students are simply known as their preferred name. Again, there can be many reasons why somebody may wish to use a name other than their legal one. It's not a hard change to make for teachers or administrators, and it makes a huge difference to be called by a name that is comfortable.

PLANNING AND RUNNING YOUR RSE LESSON BLOCKS

STEP 1

As with this book, we must start with the self and consider you the teacher. Relationships and sex are of a deeply personal and individual nature. It is natural that we each have different responses to discussion of such topics and being asked to do so professionally may feel completely out of your comfort zone. We invite you to take some time to consider this, perhaps using the following questions as a guide to understand just how you feel about delivering RSE.

- Are there any specific personal barriers when you think about your own gender, sexual identity, relationships or feelings around sex that are prominent for you?
- If there are particular areas of discomfort or any other type of feeling, can you locate exactly what that is about – e.g. this could be connected to a specific experience or religious belief or health matter, and so on.
- How well equipped and supported do you feel to deliver RSE at your education setting?
- Can you identify any doubts or fears around the potential response to your delivery of RSE?

There are many more possible questions or factors to consider, and we ask you to do so, because your feelings and personal boundaries are important. There would be something fundamentally wrong about any individual being forced to deliver education against their will, as we consider in Chapter 6 when we think about policy. It might be that a school decides to have one or two 'leads' on delivering RSE, which they do not deliver to their own class. It needs to work for the school and for teachers to feel comfortable and competent (even if they are not entirely confident). We've all done this many times before; it is a new curriculum and, with experience and support, it soon becomes second nature.

It might be that considering RSE at a greater depth has raised some personal issues for you, so that you now feel better placed to consider or perhaps to seek some advice or support. It is very common for people to remain silent on matters of relationships and sex, as the more sensitive 'difficult' or 'embarrassing' issues are often not socially acceptable to discuss openly. Take care of yourself, as number one priority, and address the issues or questions as you see fit.

STEP 2

If and when you feel ready to deliver your first Lesson in Love & Understanding, choose what you are going to cover for the lesson and give consideration to making it as accessible as possible for everybody in the group or class. This might mean that you have a teaching assistant deliver some one-to-one support, or you might group children accordingly. Remember to be mindful when doing this. What assumptions are you making about gender, maturity and the family or home backgrounds that your students are coming from? It might be (see Chapter 6 on policy) that, depending on the content of the topic, you have agreed as a school that parents have information sent out preceding lessons or sent home following lessons, so they can support the classroom learning from home. Many schools do this anyway with other subjects, so it's great planning to ensure that you have those materials ready and appropriately timed according to your school policy.

We would suggest that you try to deliver your course content using the order in which we have given our themes in Chapters 1–5 of this book. Chapters 6, 7 and 8 are more about what you will implement at the staff, management and school policy level. They are ordered last in the book, as it makes sense to consider the bulk of the content and recommendations for good practice before you think about what you need to cover and how best to integrate that to improve inclusion and RSE in your school.

STEP 3

Setting the tone and environment produces far greater results. Ideally, sessions should run over half-term blocks, covering one 60-minute slot per week. Pick your timing so that where possible, the class can take a 5-minute break in the middle of the session, where they can get a drink, use the toilet, move around and get some fresh air. Be mindful that with any social education sessions, we cannot assume what is going on for any individual, and we need this space to feel manageable, teaching in bite-sized chunks, and also to allow the discrete opportunity for questions and the teacher to organise a safe ending to the lesson.

Set your classroom in as comfortable an arrangement as possible. Some schools have cushions and soft floor furnishings for 'carpet time'; for older age groups, it might be that moving chairs and tables around is best for whatever you have decided to do in your lesson. Temperature is important, as hormonal pubescents can overheat easily (this can cause discomfort or potentially fainting), so try to keep the room cool and airy, and have water to hand. We also like to use grounding activities, such as mindful colouring or themed activity sheets if much time is to be spent sitting listening to the teacher during the lesson, as it can be helpful for those feeling over- or underwhelmed to tune in. Please see our Additional resources section for links.

STEP 4

At the beginning of the lesson state very clearly what you are going to be covering and indicate the time that each section will run for, including the all-important break.

Outline the rules for engagement with your class, emphasising respect, trust and confidentiality. Usually groups are happy to set these rules or contracts using their own suggestions and with helpful facilitation. It is important to state that there may be people in class who are affected by some of the topics discussed and we never know what somebody or their family may be going through, so we should always be sensitive to this.

It is also always good to explain from the start that discussing the topic can be embarrassing, or funny, or cringe-worthy, or a number of things, and that whatever people's feelings and opinions are, it is all right if they are being respectful towards others.

Offer everybody in the group/class a slip of paper and pencil, and ask that before the break they write down a question or something that has not been covered in the lesson that they would like to know more about. Explain that you will collect them in a bucket anonymously before the break so that you can check to see whether there are areas to cover before the end of the session, and then try to deal with them.

STEP 5

Enjoy the session with the students and have fun with it. See the box for our top tips on dealing with tricky situations. Keep strictly to time and, after collecting the slips of paper, invite students to take a 5–10-minute break.

STEP 6

Take a break. In this time, sort through the slips and write on the board any key questions or themes that come up. When the students return from their break, you can explain that other areas will be covered in future sessions. Prepare the room for the next part of your plan and, if possible, put a small token of love on each student's place. Ideas can be a small pebble or shell (symbolising the beauty of being unique), a chocolate or sweet, some fruit or a biscuit (simply because it's an enjoyable sensory experience and there's nothing like a good dopamine reward to keep pupils motivated). The gesture changes the dynamic in the room and helps pupils to feel valued and welcome in the space.

STEP 7

Start back with a welcome and explain at what point you will address some of the questions/points. Continue with the lesson as planned, inserting the questions as you feel appropriate to keep the attention of your group. Try not to end the session on questions, but rather with celebrating the class's willingness to work with this new topic in a loving and respectful manner. Even if the lesson does not go exactly as you hoped, there are always positives to reinforce and take away from the session. Draw the session to a close on a celebratory note and let the class know when to expect the next session, giving handouts where appropriate.

STEP 8

It is great if you can buddy-up with colleagues, as well as teaching RSE for peer support and shared ideas. It might be that you have a group of teachers who teach RSE to one another's regular class groups, and this makes it especially helpful to get together in a structured way. Integrative counselling therapists call it peer or group supervision. There are different ways to structure this, and you can arrange it to suit the needs of your group, taking into consideration time constraints. There is also no need to have every group member there (so if only two out of seven of you can make it one week, that's fine). Normally, in a place of work, you might have an email group and appoint two or three people to bring a situation to the group and rotate for each session. Each individual has time to present their case. It can be something they found awkward in RSE, an ethical dilemma, or a scenario that played out that they would like different viewpoints on – anything they would like to bring, including success stories to share. The person presenting then asks the group for the feedback, advice, opinions or support they would like. This is not a space for criticism and should be a supportive place where everybody can learn from the sharing of experience in a confidential and professional way. It can be helpful to have a group participant who is not presenting to facilitate and keep time, as sometimes scenarios involve lots of background and detail that can take too long and may not all be relevant. Of course, the usual codes of confidentiality apply, and teachers must only share names and other details of their students on a need-to-know basis. For group-supervision purposes, it is rarely necessary to name children at all, as it is focused on the practice of the professional. Group supervision is not a place for safeguarding cases. However, should a case be brought to group supervision that is deemed to be so, then discussion must be discontinued immediately and the case should go through the appropriate safeguarding procedures. As with any group of this nature, you contract at the beginning of each session for your agreed rules (which might change according to who attends each group).

Immediately at the beginning and directly at the end of each group-supervision session, a grounding exercise is a therapeutic way of bringing focus mindfully to the present (at the start) and disrobing from the process (at the end), prepared to step back out of the group, free of burden and distraction. Some groups choose to do one or the other, and also to have a check-in or check-out, whereby each group member says a little about how they are feeling, either going into the session or on leaving the session. Learning and taking turns to lead grounding exercises is a fantastic transferable skill that can be used in all group settings – perfect for the classroom. You can be creative with this, using movement, meditation, reflective poetry or prose, guided visualisation, mindfulness, and you can raise energy or create calm based on a sense of what the group need at any time. Further guidance on this can be found in the Additional resources at the end of the chapter and also online at: wwwlessonsinlove.info

Here is a sample script of how a supervision group might be facilitated:

A group of five teachers arrive from end-of-day administrative tasks, pull chairs into a circle and make themselves comfortable with water or coffee to hand. Pre-arranged by email, five of eight teachers are able to attend. They have self-nominated that T2 and T3 are going to present and T1 will facilitate this week. The group has 60 minutes and the facilitator will keep time, so both T2 and T3 have a fair chance for their presentation, questions to the group and responses.

T1: Welcome everybody. I'd like to invite you to join me for a grounding exercise to start the session. If we can start on our feet and have a good shake out of all the stresses and strains of the day, shaking our hands, arms, heads, bodies, legs, feet and feeling a sense of any negativity leaving our bodies. Now if I can ask you sit comfortably, with both feet rooted to the floor, arms relaxed, I am going to talk you through a mindful body-scan visualisation (continues for a maximum of 5 minutes). Now gently bring your attention back to the room, becoming aware of your feet still rooted to the floor. Is there anything anybody would like to share with the group before we have the first presentation?

T5: Thank you, I would just like to share that my dog died this morning and I'm feeling very sad having had to hold it together all day, so I may appear more emotional than usual today, and that's why.

(T1–T4 all offer condolences)

T1: Is there anything you need from the group to feel supported right now?

T5: No, thank you, it's kind of you all to care and I feel better having told you.

T4: Does anybody mind if I eat during this session, as I'm feeling very hungry?

(All other teachers agree that the group should eat and drink to feel comfortable.)

T1: OK, well, if T2 or T3 would like to pick who starts, can we hear the first presentation, please, and I'll keep you to time so we have questions and support before moving on to the next presentation?

(Presentations and questions to group, support, feedback and conversation from group.)

T1: OK, everybody, we are coming to the end of our session and I'd just like to check that everybody is satisfied with what we have covered in our discussion today.

(All say they are happy.)

T1: As we are just about at time, could I ask that we go around the group and check out using three words that describe how you are feeling right now?

T2: Relieved, supported, encouraged.

T3: Happy, motivated, inspired.

T4: Thoughtful, insightful, excited.

T5: Exhausted, sad, supported.

T1: Grateful, appreciative, honoured (leaves silence for reflective space). Thank you everybody. Can we agree a time, date and facilitator for the next meeting?

T3: I'm happy to facilitate. Is two weeks' time OK, to give the others a chance of making it rather than waiting a month, and I'll email out to see who would like to present a case?

(Other teachers agree this is fine.)

T1: Perfect. Thanks everybody. Feel free to do as you need to do now before you leave this space. Go well, take care and well done us for excellent RSE work, team!

The eight steps we have outlined above are summarised in Figure 7.1.

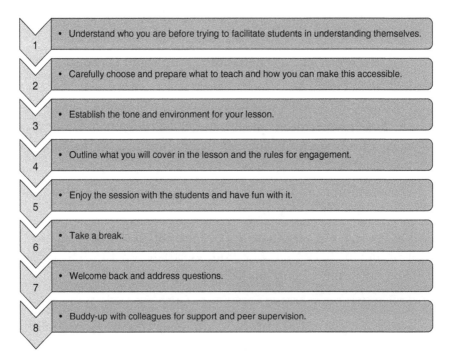

Figure 7.1 The eight-step model for teaching RSE

With all areas of education, our preparation and planning is essential for what goes into each lesson. Time constraints often mean that we neglect what happens beyond the lesson. Teachers systematically review and ask for feedback to inform on lessons identified and useful information for moving forwards. The focus on student welfare is great. But what about the teachers' welfare? Teachers, educators and parents go into their roles of learning provision as real living human beings, with their own relationship and sex stories, and the various implications of that past, present and future. In any kind of social education, one must protect that and have a curious awareness of what belongs to self and what belongs to other. Part of the criticisms being faced by primary schools, including all gender and sexualities in RSE, is that there is some kind of personal biased agenda being thrust upon young children. Some teachers who have advocated LGBTQI+ have been accused of bringing their own social political stance into the classroom, in order to somehow legitimise their personal relationship multiplicities. As the authors of this book, and people who have had lots of personal and professional therapy to examine our own blind-spots and motivations, we stand firm in saying that our motivation is in fair education, and championing equality and diversity. As professionals who are also human beings, we continue to have regular, structured conversations around our work, as well as private external supervision. This is all about remaining unbiased, grounded and healthy, and is part of good practice that allows us to think clearly about what we say and do. Inevitably, these conversations touch on personal matters, which is important. We all need safe and boundaried places to take this stuff. Everybody has different levels of what they are comfortable disclosing with colleagues, even if those colleagues are also friends. So, booking counselling therapy to use for professional supervision can be a great option. You may be curious about what might come up for a teacher in therapy. Anything is possible, as is the nature of human beings and counselling therapy. Here are some voices of educators about their experience of supervision:

> Teaching RSE is not especially in my comfort zone. I spoke to colleagues about how they felt and got the sense I was more concerned and stressed-out about it than most. I found it embarrassing to talk about, so booked a counsellor. As I spoke, I realised that I felt out of my depth, as I've never been particularly sexual or interested in sex myself. I've never considered labelling myself in terms of sexual or gender identity, but now I'm learning more, it's reassuring to know that there are lots of people like me out there, and it doesn't make me, or them, less entitled to a happy relationship. The self-learning has enabled me to build my own self-confidence and my ability running RSE lessons is far greater. (Kabirah, age 36)

At one point in my career, I was full-time teaching at the same time as I was coping with the breakdown of a 28-year marriage, whereby I was discovering infidelity after infidelity, several different partners, including people I knew and thought were friends. Teaching RSE was too close to the bone for me; but actually, there were lots of triggers hurting my heart in the day-to-day school life and I needed to somehow get on with my job, which I have always loved. I spoke to my GP who arranged counselling in a centre where I also had some massage and reflexology. It helped me manage my stress and to separate my personal and professional experiences, as I knew I had somewhere I was getting support with the hurt I was experiencing. I enjoy delivering RSE and social education nowadays. (Zola, age 55)

Kabirah and Zola's examples show that there can be a number of reasons relating to personal identity or experiences that mean we must protect ourselves so we are in a safe place to engage fully and mindfully with RSE. Part of the fear in delivering RSE in the classroom is that as teachers and educators we feel a responsibility for the many different dynamics potentially at play for each individual. There is also the unspoken pressure of being a role model to our students. Before we dwell on that concept for too long, remember: it is your own self-care, boundaries and self-respect that you are modelling just perfectly. Here are a trusty set of tools for those more challenging situations.

SCENARIO A: THE PERSONAL QUESTION

Student asks teacher/parent a personal question such as 'Do you have a boyfriend?' or 'Do you have oral sex?'

REASON

Ask yourself, with any such question, is it in the benefit of the student/class and their education to know the answer?

RESPONSE SUGGESTIONS

1. Let us think about what we really want or need to know with those questions. If I give you information based on any one person, including me, it does not provide you with useful information about the rest of society. I might tell you I have a preference for

dressing up as a space cadet and miming the moon landing in my spare time, but it doesn't mean that's what all adults of my age do. How might we turn that into a more general, less personal and specific question?

2. Thanks for your question, and all respectful questions are good ones, as are respectful answers. I don't expect any of you to share anything deeply personal with me or the class, and I similarly have my own boundaries. So, here is a great opportunity to think about our own boundaries. All of us will get asked many questions in our lives, and we have a responsibility to clearly communicate our response. Choosing not to answer a question is a valid response that can be clearly communicated in a respectful way. Let's think and talk about that.

SCENARIO B: THE RELIGIOUS/MORAL DEBATE

Student states that identifying as LGBTQI+ is wrong and that it is against their belief systems and their family's too, and they believe that somebody identifying as such will go to hell or not be accepted by their family.

REASON

Ask yourself what it is that this student needs in making the statement. Try to locate where the fear is within the statement and decide whether this is something that would be appropriate for a one-to-one conversation, as well as addressing in class.

RESPONSE SUGGESTIONS

1. It is very important for us to recognise that we all have different belief systems, and come from different cultures and backgrounds. No two people in this school will share exactly the same set of beliefs, regardless of what religion you might be, or if you are from the same family, or if you are fanatical about the same cultural or interest group. We have to appreciate that some families have strict family rules about conforming to certain ideologies, and this is OK. So long as families cause one another no harm and we all stick to our school rules of respecting others that may or may not have some of the same beliefs as us, we can all live and learn peacefully side by side.

2. The classroom is somewhere safe to share your beliefs and have freedom of speech. The only restrictions on this are when actions or words are malicious, harmful or offensive towards any other person (that person does not need to be in the room for offence to be directed at any one group of people). If behaviour is legal and respectful, it is healthy to talk about and consider different belief systems and all learn more about one another.

SCENARIO C: MANAGING EMBARRASSMENT AND PREVENTING SHAME

Inevitably, regardless of what age and stage you are teaching, you will have at least one student per session who says something in a group (perhaps outside of the actual lesson) or asks a question that is deemed by peers to be shamefully inappropriate and/or lacking in knowledge on RSE. For example, a 14-year-old not knowing what a period is or a 6-year-old disclosing that they had viewed their parents' pornography. The class may respond in shock, laughter or sniggering.

REASON

How can this situation be managed in a way that minimises harm and shame? You are likely to know if the child in question has a learning or behavioural need which makes their response fairly typical in terms of their understanding. Make a calm judgement of the class response. Are they mocking the student? Are there any wider child protection concerns?

RESPONSE SUGGESTIONS

1. OK, students, can we please revisit our code of conduct for how we are going to be in this group? Can anybody please suggest what would have been a more sensible and respectful response to what your classmate said? If not, let me help you out . . .

2. We all have very different ways of learning and the idea is that school helps you to do that, as otherwise this is all one big guessing game, and we will all get in a muddle and learn things from stuff we see on television or online. We need to be careful not to do that, and parents and carers must help us all in our understanding of life, love and relationships, otherwise it's easy to get the wrong ideas.

SCENARIO D: THE COMPLICATED QUESTION

Sometimes students ask questions that are too complex for a clear answer. For example: 'So is being a transvestite about sex, but being a trans woman about gender, and are both a choice or not?'

REASON

This type of question shows that a student is really engaging with the topic and is searching for a deeper level of understanding. Although this is a difficult question, it's important to nurture it, and also to give an unbiased and intelligent response.

RESPONSE SUGGESTIONS

1. This is a really good question and people have differing experiences of identifying as trans or a transvestite. Let's consider both and try to define the differences as a group (use the Glossary to help).
2. 'Choice' is such an interesting word, as there are many different implications and motivations behind our choices. Let's consider the different types of life choices we make and why, before looking at the definitions of transvestite and trans woman, as this is such a great question for our discussion.

In Chapter 8 there is further discussion around the debates and issues that tend to come up around RSE in order to give clarification in managing topics such as choice, ethics and morality.

The take-away lessons from this chapter are for your staff team. We are only too aware of teacher time poverty, and we need this to be realistic. So, we have timetabled for you how this might fit into your planning schedule to try to make it happen.

1. At the next staff meeting opportunity, put in minutes to discuss whether somebody is going to take the lead for RSE and whether all the teachers are going to run these lessons, or a group, or two/a few people. If two/a few people, can they have some time allocated to prepare and their classes covered as they deliver the lessons for every class. It should not be down to just one person in case they become ill or for some reason cannot deliver, and then there is no proper RSE provision.

2. The RSE team – hopefully self-appointed and enthusiastic volunteers – should then set a 20-minute meeting date. Everyone must request a copy of this book and read it before the agreed meeting time. If you are on the team, welcome! You will not regret becoming a subject matter expert in this field. Consider yourself a pioneer and trail-blazer in this crucial area of teaching.

3. At your 20-minute meeting, decide how you are going to split the teaching, how many sessions for each class and what you are going to cover. This should not take longer than 20 minutes as it is just the practical side of making sure this is in the planner so that these lessons happen.

4. Each individual can then work alone in their own time, deciding what they are going to deliver to whom, and then working out what resources need to be organised or sourced for the classes, so they each have the suggested recommended reading and literature.

5. Email the RSE team and arrange an initial group supervision session. For this initial session, rather than two or three people presenting, ask everybody to have some questions prepared about RSE, and in the session, take it in turns to ask your questions and then discuss. The first session should allow 1 hour minimum. As a one-off, 2 hours is a really great way to collect your ideas and feel supported and confident in delivering RSE with the new requirements, and gives time to address any issues. Agree a date for your first supervision session beyond this initial meeting, once you have started the RSE teaching. Contract for the possibility of peer support in between sessions in a way that is practical for you all. And enjoy!

KEY POINTS

- Consider your personal self. Your feelings and personal boundaries are important. Are there any personal barriers that are prominent for you?
- Create loving spaces through using inclusive language, being conscious not to make assumptions about gender and sexuality, to represent all styles of family life and break free of the heteronormative narrative when interacting with students and staff.
- Preparation and planning are the key to success, as they are in any area of teaching.

- Consider the resources and support you need for facilitating RSE in your setting.
- Ensure that you have a long-term and medium-term plan for the block of RSE you will be teaching.
- Assess the class to ensure that your teaching is appropriate to their level.
- Make a detailed lesson plan prior to delivery. This will help provide you with a framework while considering possible alternatives as the lesson progresses.
- Ensure that the room is comfortable (seating, temperature, etc.) and also that breaks are built into the lesson.
- Outline the expectations for the lesson: what will be covered, how students should engage, respect, trust, confidentiality.
- Have your resources ready such as slips of paper for questions, a question box, a treat.
- Support and share ideas with colleagues, either within your school or within a network.
- Enjoy teaching the session.

ADDITIONAL RESOURCES

No further resources are recommended for this chapter as we would trust that this book contains sufficient information.

A range of resources are available to help you look after your own well-being – for example:

- The Education Support Partnership: www.educationsupport partnership.org.uk. This contains a range of useful information and additional signposting, while also including their recent 'Teacher Wellbeing Index': www.educationsupportpartnership. org.uk/sites/default/files/teacher_wellbeing_index_2018.pdf
- Britain Get Talking: www.itv.com/britaingettalking/
- Mental Health Foundation: www.mentalhealth.org.uk/
- Please also look at the supporting website for this book: www.les sonsinlove.info

8

ETHICS, ADVOCACY AND WHO DOES WHAT

CONTENTS

- Why this chapter?
- Boundaries
- A guide to providing guidance and support
- Lessons in love and understanding for professional development

CHAPTER OBJECTIVES

- To appreciate the need to establish professional boundaries.
- To understand the three steps and five tips for providing guidance and support.
- To identify a range of issues and how these may be resolved within the wider context.

WHY THIS CHAPTER?

In our final chapter, we have the small matter of trying to cover everything else you may still have questions about in this broad and exciting topic. Being 'The RSE Teacher' and appointed Subject Matter Expert on teaching this subject is only a daunting task if you allow it to be. No individual can possibly be held solely accountable for the RSE of any other. In providing effective education, there is shared and collective responsibility. In terms of our personal responsibilities in teaching this subject, the most important thing is what we do, as opposed to the pre-2020 approach to inclusive RSE: if in doubt, do nothing. As with the teaching of any subject, we learn and alter and evolve as is appropriate to be effective in providing the best education we can, but this has to start somewhere. Our hope is that by this stage in the book, you are feeling more confident and relaxed about teaching all-inclusive RSE. As we said from the start, you already have all the skills you need in order to approach this subject. In Chapter 6 we looked at applying the British Government guidelines in a meaningful way. Chapter 7 went on to provide a step-by-step guide to delivering a well-held RSE lesson. In this final chapter, we aim to provide you with some external back-up, so that you are not in isolation delivering these lessons, as a school, teacher or parent. We have deliberately left this information until last because the book is about enabling you as a teacher. However, now you know you can deliver these lessons with excellence, the great news is that there is further support out there.

BOUNDARIES

One of the most central themes to the teaching of any kind of social education, and particularly RSE, is boundaries. The word (including the term 'boundaried') has been used 32 times throughout this book because it is so important in every aspect of protecting ourselves and other people we come into contact with, be that personally, professionally or otherwise. Also discussed in several other chapters is our mission to protect and preserve the teacher, your sense of self and sanity. Teachers are over-burdened enough. So, first may we invite you to try an exercise in looking at roles and responsibilities.

Below is a table for you to fill in the different jobs you see as attached to RSE (Table 8.1). Number the roles in order of responsibility – with 1 as main responsibility and 3 as low-level responsibility if jobs apply to more than one area. As you answer the questions, please be mindful that there are no firm right or wrong answers – this is about looking at the boundaries within your role. We are not including parents in this table of responsibility, as we take it as fact that parents do have responsibilities at every level. We have started filling this table out as an example of how a secondary school teacher might approach it to get you started.

Table 8.1 Different jobs attached to RSE

Job	My role	Somebody else's role (name)	School management role
Teaching about safe internet use and the dangers of grooming.	1. A clear part of my role.	1. All teachers share this role as everybody is teaching this.	2. School management ensures that appropriate training can be accessed by teachers, parents, carers and students.
Providing emergency contraception and advice.	3. I might need to signpost but it is not my responsibility.	School nurse? 1. GP CAMHS?	3. May need to signpost?
Supporting a student with gender dysphoria in class.			
Please continue with the type of roles you might come across with children you educate and think about who is responsible for which job and in which role.			

As you can see, it is not clear-cut. We are sure that many of you will also have experienced that you are often the first point of contact for all the many types of support, advice and help requested and required by families belonging to your school. Primary school headteacher Nicole describes her experience of feeling responsible for the well-being of one family who sought her support:

> It's not unusual for parents to arrange to see me to discuss what they initially describe as a personal matter. As a school we welcome this as it's important we know about anything that families feel significant to tell us. When the parents of a Year 2 student came to tell me that Mum was socially transitioning and identified as male, I was quite taken a back. I felt out of my depth as I wasn't familiar with the terminology the parents were using to tell me about this, and I didn't really know what school could or should do to support. I asked the parents if there was anything specific I or school could do. They asked what advice I had on making this easier for their child at the time when other school families and classmates became aware of the transition. Quite frankly, I didn't have a clue. So, I arranged a follow up meeting with the promise I would take some advice and come back to them on this matter. (Nicole, age 40)

Nicole did the right thing, as under the circumstances she did not have the training or knowledge of how to best support the family in this situation. Here we will provide you with a step-by-step guide on how you can provide instant support when required. We will also suggest resources that you may build up into a well-being library, for your school or in your own professional literature collection.

A GUIDE TO PROVIDING GUIDANCE AND SUPPORT

Step 1 Create time and space to really listen to what the student or family that have chosen to talk to you have to say. Make no assumptions and ask open questions for clarity if this helps your understanding. When you ask questions, do keep in mind that it is on a need-to-know basis in order to support in your role. The student or family may disclose whatever they wish, but it is important that you only ask questions that have the student's best interest at heart. The key questions to have in mind are:

- How is or might the situation you are learning of impact on the student's well-being either directly or indirectly?
- What is the purpose of the student or family disclosing this information to you? What are their hopes for how you or school might respond – i.e. are they looking for support or are they giving you information so that you are aware of a situation without this necessarily requiring any action?
- Who is concerned with this matter? Are there other students implicated within the matter – for example, in romantic or sexual relationships – and/or are there outside agencies also involved?
- How might the issue impact on the student's education? For example, teen pregnancy or surgery that some trans teens may seek may have an impact on time out of school and the need to change the structure of learning.
- Is there a child protection matter or an issue that requires specific school attention, and are there other agencies involved?
- What kind of support network does the student and family have?

Ask the student or family if you may take some notes in order that you have a full understanding of the situation (where this is appropriate). Thank the student or family for sharing with you and recount your understanding of what the student or family have told you to ensure that you understood correctly. You can then ask specifically how you and school might support.

Step 2 In responding to requests for support, be mindful of the earlier exercise in finding a safe balance between taking responsibility for the part you can play in supporting without over-burdening yourself and sharing responsibility with others. The next exercise is one that is massively helpful in looking at all support plans. It is a great CPD exercise as a team, to look at your local resources, and it is also fantastic to do with a group of students or one to one with an individual, so that people are aware of the resources of support they have and where to go for help. In British culture there is fear around us becoming a nation of dependants, reliant on a welfare state that is overwhelmed and underfunded. As teachers, if we can support students in building resilience by providing tools for self-nurture, we are enabling people and communities through sustainable education for adulthood – for example, please refer to the work of Cathie Freeman in the Additional resources at the end of the chapter.

Table 8.2 below can be used in many different ways. We have given the example of how this might be filled in by a pupil in a Year 9 class in Cornwall, who has been asked by the teacher to fill in the resources somebody might turn to if they were feeling extremely depressed and confused about their gender and sexuality. Collectively, the class can feed back to the teacher so a huge possible resource list can be made. The teacher can then provide extra resources (using our suggestions and from their own local research) which the example below shows in italics.

Table 8.2 Resourcing support

Short-term	Medium-term	Long-term
GP	GP	Family and/or friends
Teacher or Year Head	School Counsellor	Church/faith community
Online support groups	CAMHS	Online support groups
Youth worker	Online support groups	Community support groups
Go to Pride event	YAY South West/intercom	YAY South West/intercom
Terrence Higgins Trust	Pink Therapy	Pink Therapy
GIRES	LGBTQ Home – Barnardo's	Rainbow families
Young Stonewall	Mermaids UK	
The Trevor Project		

The list will go on and on when you take the knowledge of the class, and then do your own local research to see what is available specifically for your area. Just knowing that support is available can be of great comfort and provide a safety net for challenging times, plus resources to prevent isolation. As teachers, we spend a lot of time safeguarding against the dangers of the internet. Happily, there are huge educational benefits when it is used responsibly. Creating this type of resource list can, of course, be useful with any element of health education.

Step 3 Don't forget that you are part of a team. If you are home schooling, it is good practice to have a network in place to support you and your children in learning, so do utilise this. With RSE we are often dealing in sensitive and private matters, and one must absolutely adhere to policy in confidentiality and in child protection. However, let us not get so bogged down that we do not communicate with our teams in order that intelligent, informed and ethical decisions are made. If, as educators, we can talk about difficult topics, and have an open and balanced discussion and debate about emotive and contentious subjects, learning will be greatly enriched, and the modelling of this healthy communication will infiltrate throughout our places of education. RSE 2020 is about progression and we can only progress by working together. This is an interesting paradox, as what we have been talking about in this book is our uniqueness as human beings. Being individual and unique, however, means that there is not one right way of doing things. Every ethical dilemma you might face in any situation or issue that you are asked to 'deal with' as an educator will have many possible responses or ways of working out. By collective thinking and discussion in sharing our thoughts and ideas we give the highest possible likelihood of responding to any individual scenario in a helpful way.

Collaborative working might take many forms. Peer supervision is a great way to start in-house looking at various ethical dilemmas and considering different issues and ideas that come up in everyday teaching practice. Team meetings can also be a valuable opportunity to address matters of policy, procedures and changes that are to be implemented in teaching in response to the needs of students and their well-being. Multidisciplinary team meetings are, again, so helpful in allowing different aspects of a student's educational needs to be viewed from alternative perspectives. This information can be key to understanding and relating to a student, and the best way to support them in learning. Wider welfare multi-agency meetings, where professionals from outside the school are invited to attend to represent their work with a family/student, are also invaluable in what joined-up working can achieve when communication links are strong. Schools should not be shy in inviting other agencies to discuss student welfare where appropriate, as this collaborative working is of mutual benefit to all and avoids overlap and repetition.

Step 4 Delegate advocacy to the Subject Matter Experts in the appropriate organisations relating to the cause at hand. We expect that you are already providing advocacy for every single student that you teach, on an everyday basis, in that you represent the needs and voices of your students in everything you do to meet their educational needs.

As we have said throughout this book, there is so much that you are already doing in your role as a teacher and in your individual relationships and understanding of each of your student's needs. You are one of their main supporters and advocates, so do signpost, using our links if you are not sure where.

Step 5 Professional learning and development need not be costly or dull. Some of the best learning is in the sharing of experience and working towards solutions and planning as a professional group. The phrase 'every day's a school day' is so true for every living being, as we are constantly learning and applying what we learn to how we engage and interact with others. So, the following Lessons in Love and Understanding are for you, the educators, as another well-used phrase is also true: 'practice makes perfect'.

These five steps are summarised in Figure 8.1.

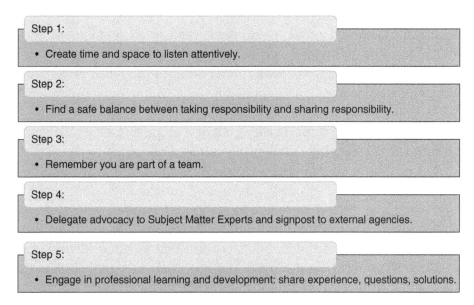

Step 1:
  • Create time and space to listen attentively.

Step 2:
  • Find a safe balance between taking responsibility and sharing responsibility.

Step 3:
  • Remember you are part of a team.

Step 4:
  • Delegate advocacy to Subject Matter Experts and signpost to external agencies.

Step 5:
  • Engage in professional learning and development: share experience, questions, solutions.

Figure 8.1   A guide for providing guidance and support

LESSONS IN LOVE AND UNDERSTANDING FOR PROFESSIONAL DEVELOPMENT

1. Create some cards with different scenarios that a student might disclose to a teacher. Hand out the cards to different members of the group. Ask the person with the card to role play the scenario

and a volunteer to be the teacher in this role play. The rest of the group are there to support the teacher in the role play. Every time the teacher would like some guidance on how to react, they pause the role play by turning to look at their colleagues who must work as a group to figure out the best response to the 'student'. It might be that the person in the 'teacher' role manages the situation without guidance, in which case, bring to the discussion as many ideas as possible on different ways of handling the scenario, discussing potential problems.

2. Prepare the debate: for and against all-inclusive LGBTQI+ RSE at primary school. Play out this debate as well as you can in order to bring insight into differing fears and views about teaching young people about relationships and sex.

3. Create two teams and set each other a quiz on RSE facts, including history, law, policy and terminology. Swap papers to answer and each team go through the correct answers to the questions together. This is fun team learning and sharing of knowledge, and highlights areas for swatting up where there is a lack of knowledge.

4. Choose any of the class exercises that you are interested in and try them out as a group to share the classroom experience. Role play as you wish to highlight any potential challenges and gain experience in the opportunity to practise.

5. For a whole-school approach, a staff development session could be devoted to assigning small groups an area on which to develop a poster, quiz or presentation. This in turn could lead to 'the mantle of the expert'. For example, the area of 'protected characteristics' could be identified from the Equality Act (2010), with groups spending an hour finding out information about the area, how the characteristic is defined, and facts and figures, then identifying three steps the school already engages with as a model of best practice while identifying one more strategy that could be engaged in the wider context.

Having started this book by taking a look at self-identity, it feels fitting to end in looking at the wider context, addressing RSE within some of the more general topics that are widely discussed concerning health and well-being. In order to do this, we have collected some teachers' voices that represent some of the more common questions we are asked as sexperts.

I've been teaching for 25 years and I don't understand how only in the last 5 of those years there are so many students claiming to have gender issues. It doesn't seem that this can honestly be the case for all of these kids, but we daren't challenge this in risk of offending and being struck-off work by the PC-police. It's not just transgender, it's also self-harm, and if I'm honest . . . it often feels as though it is the trendy thing to have some kind of mental health issue or carry some kind of label that puts you in a subset of students who then demand special rights and attention. What is the best way to manage this in order that the students who really do need the support do receive it, and so that classes aren't completely disrupted by students claiming they are not mentally well enough to be in class? (Angela, age 52)

The fear from this teacher is that there are students confusing or faking gender or mental health concerns, or perhaps both, and that this detracts attention away from the students who really do need the extra support, as well as interfering with the delivery of lessons through the disruption this causes in class. The copy-cat phenomenon has been widely discussed in terms of suicide and self-harm, and, in our understanding, it is the method of expression that may be inspired or imitated, rather than the core thoughts, beliefs and feelings behind the action. So, in the case of the pupil who seems to copy their best mate in identifying as trans and dressing in a similar style, they are likely to have already felt that they were trans, and felt inspired by their friend's expression of their gender identity so experimented to see if this also felt fitting for them. We know that humans don't tend to continue or repeat behaviours unless those behaviours are serving us in some way. For example, somebody self-harming through cutting and scratching might find that the feeling of adrenaline and release this gives them is a temporary remedy to the numbness and depression they are living with daily. The cutting and scratching is actually a remedy to the mental torment they are otherwise enduring, so is therefore helpful to them. Nobody would choose the pain, bleeding, scars and risk of infection or haemorrhage as some kind of fashion statement or to fit in with their friends. Similarly, transition of any kind is not a comfortable thing to do. People do not go through this for fun or as a lifestyle choice. Providing opportunity for safe and structured conversations and education around health and well-being in a fully inclusive way is the best way to know you are providing opportunity for everybody to access the correct amount of support that they require on an individual basis. It is not your job, as a teacher, to make any judgements or decisions on who requires what. This would be an impossible task and could have disastrous consequences.

It is sometimes hard to know, however, just where to draw the line in terms of school involvement. Here we have another teacher's voice to help explore this type of dilemma:

> We knew at school that social services were involved with one of our families, and it was rumoured that the mother was working as a **prostitute** and the eldest sibling was also making a living from internet sex work from home. The younger siblings were Key Stage 2 at our school. Knowing Social Services were in touch with the family meant we did not need to be directly involved with this case, unless we became privy to further information which we would then pass on to them as appropriate with our safeguarding policy. However, as class teacher of one of the children I couldn't help but wonder how safe the child was and how much Social Services could possibly know. I was curious about the level of stress on the younger siblings and what they may be having to conceal so that their mum and big sister didn't get into trouble. To me, this was my concern as a teacher, and I kept a close eye on those children. (Robyn, age 27)

It is not uncommon to have some background information that is uncertain and perhaps deemed not to be a school matter. However, it is useful to keep this information in mind as a possibility when working with the students concerned. An awareness of the possibilities and the various backgrounds that come with any one class of pupils enables the educator to be mindful about what is delivered in class. It's important to check out the class concepts of safety and how safety can mean different things to different people. It might be that your team decide that RSE at your school should include teaching around internet safety and the realities of the sex industry from Key Stage 2. It absolutely makes sense that you respond, as a school, to the social problems your school sees as affecting your catchment area and your wider school community. Joint work with the police and tapping into their specific training on issues such as sex work and sex trafficking, domestic violence, female genital mutilation and hate crime is invaluable in aiding the educator's understanding of these very serious issues and how we can work together as communities in a multi-agency way to protect against and support those vulnerable to such situations.

It is always worth checking at any multi-agency meeting that you have what training others might be able to offer to your teachers and/ or workshops for the pupils. Community Education teams provide a great number of health-related workshops, as do many charities. You will normally find that there is a charity response to specific issues that affect localities and that an important part of what they provide is educational outreach. It is such a valuable team exercise to resource pool together and share your knowledge of supporting organisations, as we cannot expect teachers to become experts at every level of RSE. In September 2019, sports personality Gareth Thomas made a public announcement that he was living with HIV. He asked for 'public support' and said he 'trusted the public' to offer this. A celebrity RSE story making world news raises new public awareness and often highlights the gaps in public knowledge. Over the years there have been great medical developments in how HIV is managed, and many people can lead full lives and never develop AIDS on controlled medication once they have received an HIV-positive diagnosis. To have teaching from a professional working in the field – for example, a medic from a **GUM clinic** or sexual health expert – adds a far deeper level of understanding for students and provides the most up-to-date information and local resource links.

Sometimes it is going to be absolutely essential that you work with a multi-agency plan, where young people have complex needs and/or SEND. Individual plans must be created through consulting all professionals involved as well as parents or guardians. A young person with trauma from sexual abuse is going to have very different learning needs from a young person with Autistic Spectrum Disorder in the way they receive any lessons, but for RSE these individual plans are going to be paramount for safeguarding. Let's hear the voice of a secondary school Special Educational Needs Coordinator (SENCO):

> Normally teaching RSE is one-to-one with the pupils I work with, but with some general rules about appropriate behaviour that we remind each class on a daily basis. I suppose the one area I find of concern is the correlation I have seen at the school I

> work in between gender identity and what we used to call Asperger's. It seems many of the children I have and currently do work with that have Aspie-type characteristics identify as trans and non-binary gender. When I ask them about this it can often seem that they don't view themselves as belonging to either the male or female stereotypes, which is fine until they start talking about vaginoplasty and taking hormones but then **binding** breasts that might grow – this kind of thing. I find that very worrying. (Frances, age 50)

Anecdotally, these are concerns we commonly hear from both parents and teachers of students on the autistic spectrum who are expressing gender discomfort. Many young people manage to find a place of comfort without needing medical intervention. However, counselling therapy and being able to talk through the thinking and emotions behind all of this can be extremely helpful. Living with ASD can be lonely and especially if one has an awareness that their communication style is inhibitive of having fulfilling relationships. One-to-one work on exploring one's sense of self, as well as some group work on learning relationship skills, can empower students with ASD to form meaningful connections with others, and raise their self-esteem and feeling of self-worth. To provide fully inclusive RSE we must consider whether there are any factors that are barriers towards the individual student forming meaningful or intimate relationships. These challenges might be psychological, psychiatric, cognitive, behavioural, physical or a combination of elements. As a teacher, it may or may not be your role to provide any type of intervention, depending on the individual situation. However, you may be the person to assess what type of support might be most appropriate for the student. More often than not, this is simply about opening up that dialogue and being able to have one-to-one private and sensitive conversations with a student about RSE and their thoughts and feelings on the subject and where they sit with this. Depending on your place of education, it may be possible to have some small groups who work on relational skills as part of primary education, specifically tailored to the shared needs of the group in building empathy, compassion, thoughtfulness and consideration of others, as well as teaching about boundaries, privacy and safety in a practical way.

What we are saying is that with RSE we must 'keep it real'. It should relate to the modern world that your students live in, and it should cover all different ways of being in relationships. It should also look at human development from birth to death, because if we don't learn about this in our school years, when do we learn about it other than through our own personal experience? So many people go undiagnosed and suffer for years with DSD, sexually transmitted diseases, sexual abuse, infertility, secret abortion, geriatric relationship and sexual health issues, and other predicaments that society as a whole are largely ignorant towards. These things have gone unnoticed by family members and loved ones, or nobody has wanted to talk about them, and so people muddle on through life with a fear of their own bodies and minds, and how they might be perceived by others.

It is not healthy that we neglect our relationships and sexual health in the way that we do. The impact is huge and the secondary effects mean that we are unable to thrive as individuals and as communities through our ignorance. Education is the only thing that can save us from this sorry state and shape a happier world, where we can each feel comfortable and confident being ourselves, and truly embrace the diversity of the human race, enjoying our similarities and differences through the realisation of our potential to love.

KEY POINTS

- Teaching is a self-improving profession: we learn, alter and evolve through the process of CPD and professional reflection. This applies to teaching RSE: we need to do something rather than nothing, otherwise we will have nothing to reflect on.
- Be aware of your own personal and professional boundaries and ensure that you look after your own physical, mental and emotional well-being.
- Truly listen to what a person says without making assumptions or promising solutions.
- Be mindful of finding a balance between taking responsibility and sharing responsibility with others.
- Work as a team and communicate effectively.

(Continued)

- Be prepared to delegate advocacy to appropriate organisations.
- Engage in professional learning and development. Check what training is available with the agencies that the school operates with – e.g. the police, community education, safeguarding boards, local advocacy and support groups, charities.
- Aim to relate RSE to the modern world in which students live.

ADDITIONAL RESOURCES

Inclusive RSE will require you to be aware of, and respond to, the varying individual needs of each student. For this reason, the following website will help to provide more general guidance.

RSE TEACHING

- Home Education (advice and support for home-schooled students): www.home-education.org.uk/
- Sexplain (an organisation that provides RSE): https://sexplain.org.uk/

LGBTQI+ SUPPORT

- GIRES (Gender Identity Research and Education Society): www.gires.org.uk/
- Mermaids (an organisation that supports gender diverse and transgender children, young people and their families): https://mermaidsuk.org.uk/
- Pink Therapy (the UK's largest independent therapy organisation working with gender and sexually diverse clients): www.pinktherapy.com/
- Young Stonewall (supporting LGBTQI+ young people to campaign for equality and fair treatment): www.youngstonewall.org.uk/

SEXUAL HEALTH

- British HIV Association: www.bhiva.org/
- Brook Advisory Centres (free, confidential sexual health advice): www.brook.org.uk/
- Family Planning Association: www.fpa.org.uk/

- National Health Sexual Health Helpline (free UK calls): www. nhs.uk/oneyou/for-your-body/sexual-health/ (or call: 0300 123 7123)
- Terrence Higgins Trust (the UK's leading HIV and sexual health charity): www.tht.org.uk/
- World Association for Sexual Health (an umbrella organisation representing sexological societies internationally): www.face book.com/WAS.org/

GENERAL SEND SUPPORT

- Autism Toolbox (a resource for Scottish schools but applicable for all schools): http://autismtoolbox.co.uk/
- Down's Syndrome Association: www.downs-syndrome.org.uk/
- National Autistic Society: www.autism.org.uk/
- Make-A-Wish Foundation (support to help children with life-limiting illness): www.make-a-wish.org.uk/
- Rainbow Trust Children's Charity (an organisation that provides support for families with a child who has a life-threatening or life-limiting illness): https://rainbowtrust.org.uk/

MENTAL WELL-BEING

- CAMHS (Childhood and Adolescent Mental Health Services): www.nhs.uk/using-the-nhs/nhs-services/mental-health-services/ child-and-adolescent-mental-health-services-camhs/
- Mind (the mental health charity): www.mind.org.uk/
- Young Minds (an organisation to help children and young people's mental well-being): https://youngminds.org.uk/
- Please also refer to the work of Cathie Freeman on empowering young people through resourcing, responsibility and resilience development: www.ordinarilyextraliving.com

ADVOCACY AND RIGHTS

- Action for Children (protecting and supporting children and young people, providing advocacy along with practical and emotional care and support): www.actionforchildren.org.uk/
- Barnardo's: www.barnardos.org.uk/
- Pathfinder International (an organisation to globally champion sexual and reproductive health and rights): www.pathfinder.org

- Childline: www.childline.org.uk/ (or call: 0800 1111)
- National Children's Bureau (an organisation to bring people and organisations together to drive change in society for a better childhood for the UK): www.ncb.org.uk/
- Government Equalities Office: www.gov.uk/government/organi sations/government-equalities-office
- MACWO (Mother and Child Welfare Organisation): www.macwo. org/
- The Children's Society (providing help and support for children who may feel scared, unloved, or unable to cope): www.childrens-society.org.uk/
- NSPCC (National Society for the Prevention of Cruelty to Children): www.nspcc.org.uk/
- UNICEF (United Nations International Children's Emergency Fund): www.unicef.org.uk/
- Women's Aid (an organisation to provide life-saving services for women and children): www.womensaid.org.uk/

REFERENCES

Allen, G. and Zayed, Y. (2019) 'Hate crime statistics: Briefing Paper No. 08537'. House of Commons Library. Available from: https://researchbrief ings.parliament.uk/ResearchBriefing/Summary/CBP-8537#fullreport (accessed: 24 August 2019).

Argyle, M. (1973/2008) *Social Encounters: Contributions to Social Interaction*. Chicago: Aldine Transaction.

Bachmann, C.L. and Gooch, B. (2017) 'LGBT in Britain: Hate crime and discrimination'. London: Stonewall. Available from: www.stonewall.org.uk/system/files/lgbt_in_britain_hate_crime.pdf (accessed: 26 August 2019).

BASW (2018) *Child trafficking in the UK: A snapshot*. Available from: https://www.basw.co.uk/system/files/resources/child%20trafficking%20uk%20 2018.pdf (accessed 26th April 2020).

Brook (2019) 'Traffic light tool'. Available from: https://legacy.brook.org.uk/our-work/the-sexual-behaviours-traffic-light-tool (accessed: 14 June 2019).

Canesco, M. (2011) 'Sex education: Americans, Britons and Canadians disagree on sex education'. Angus Reid Public Opinion. Available from: https://web.archive.org/web/20161018215345/http://angusreidglobal.com/wp-content/uploads/2011/11/2011.11.30_SexEd.pdf (accessed: 7 September 2019).

Connolly, M.D., Zervos, M.J., Barone, C.J., Johnson, C.C. and Joseph, C.L. (2016) 'The mental health of transgender youth: Advances in understanding'. *Journal of Adolescent Health*, 59 (5): 489–95.

Crissman, H.P., Berger, M.B., Graham, L.F., Dalton, V.K. (2017) 'Transgender demographics: A household probability sample of US adults, 2014'. *American Journal of Public Health*, 107 (2): 213–15.

Curtice, J., Clery, E., Perry. J, Phillips, M. and Rahim, N. (eds) (2019) 'British social attitudes: The 36th report'. London: The National Centre for Social Research. Available from: www.bsa.natcen.ac.uk/media/39358/5_bsa36_ relationships_and_gender_identity.pdf (accessed: 17 August 2019).

Department for Education (DfE) (2017) 'Policy statement: Relationships education, relationships and sex education, and personal, social, health and economic education'. Available from: https://assets.publishing.service.gov. uk/government/uploads/system/uploads/attachment_data/ file/595828/170301_Policy_statement_PSHEv2.pdf (accessed: 27 August 2019).

Department for Education (DfE) (2018) 'Explain or change: Statement of intent on the diversity of the teaching workforce – information about the activity of the co-signatories'. Available from: https://assets.publishing.service.gov.uk/government/uploads/system/uploads/attachment_data/file/747594/Additional_information_about_the_activity_of_the_co-signatories.pdf (accessed: 19 September 2019).

Department for Education (DfE) (2019) 'Statutory guidance: Relationships education, relationships and sex education (RSE) and health education'. Available from: www.gov.uk/government/publications/relationships-education-relationships-and-sex-education-rse-and-health-education (accessed: 27 August 2019).

Family Planning Association (FPA) (2011) 'Teenagers: Sexual health and behaviour factsheet'. Available from: www.fpa.org.uk/factsheets/teenagers-sexual-health-behaviour (accessed: 14 July 2019).

Government Equalities Office (2018) 'Trans people in the UK'. Available from: https://assets.publishing.service.gov.uk/government/uploads/system/uploads/attachment_data/file/721642/GEO-LGBT-factsheet.pdf (accessed: 3 August 2019).

Herman-Giddens, M.E., Slora, E.J., Wasserman, R.C., Bourdony, C.J., Bhapkar, M.V., Koch, G.G. and Hasemeier, C.M. (1997) 'Secondary sexual characteristics and menses in young girls seen in office practice: A study from the pediatric research in office settings network'. *Pediatrics*, 99 (4): 505–12.

Herman-Giddens, M.E., Steffes, J., Harris, D., Slora, E., Hussey, M., Dowshen, S.A., Wasserman, R., Serwint, J.R., Smitherman, L. and Reiter, E.O. (2012) 'Secondary sexual characteristics in boys: Data from the pediatric research in office settings network'. *Pediatrics*, 130 (5): e1058–e1068.

Hinds, D. (2019) 'Letter to Paul Whiteman'. Available from: https://assets.publishing.service.gov.uk/government/uploads/system/uploads/attachment_data/file/793973/Letter_to_NAHT_from_Damian_Hinds.pdf?_ga=2.131099087.1521039628.1566889618-310636154.1564664132 (accessed: 27 August 2019).

Home Office (2019) *Hate Crime, England and Wales, 2018 to 2019*. Available from: www.gov.uk/government/collections/hate-crime-statistics (accessed: 14 November 2019).

Legislation.gov.uk (2010) Equality Act 2010. Available from: www.legislation.gov.uk/ukpga/2010/15/contents (accessed: 29 August 2019).

Legislation.gov.uk (2014) The Education (Independent School Standards) (England) (Amendment) Regulations 2014 (No. 2374). (This is more commonly known as 'British Values'.) Available from: www.legislation.gov.uk/uksi/2014/2374/pdfs/uksi_20142374_en.pdf (accessed: 29 August 2019).

Long, R. (2019). 'Relationships and sex education in schools (England). Briefing Paper No. 06103, 11 July'. Manchester: Department for Education.

NSPCC (2019) *Statistics briefing: child sexual abuse*. Available from: https://learning.nspcc.org.uk/media/1710/statistics-briefing-child-sexual-abuse.pdf (accessed 26th April 2020).

O'Connor, P. (2014) 'Searching for the self, and other unicorns'. *Psychology Today*, 47 (6): 50–1.

Office for National Statistics (2019) 'Annual population survey 2017'. Available from: www.ons.gov.uk (accessed: 13 August 2019).

Perry, W.G. (1970) *Forms of intellectual and ethical development in the college years: A scheme*. New York: Holt, Rinehart & Winston.

Stonewall (2019a) 'The truth about trans: A Q&A for people who are hungry for real info'. Available from: www.stonewall.org.uk/truth-about-trans#trans-people-britain (accessed: 12 July 2019).

Stonewall (2019b) 'Trans key stats'. Available from: www.stonewall.org.uk/sites/default/files/trans_stats.pdf (accessed: 27 October 2019).

Sumia, M., Lindberg, N., Tyolajarvi, M. and Kaltiala-Heino, R. (2017) 'Current and recalled childhood gender identity in community youth in comparison to referred adolescents seeking sex reassignment'. *Journal of Adolescence*, 56, 34–9.

Synott, A. (2016) '10 models of our self: Unicorns, chameleons, icebergs'. *Psychology Today*. Available from: www.psychologytoday.com/us/blog/rethinking-men/201607/10-models-our-self (accessed: 11 August 2019).

Todd, M. (2019) *Pride: The Story of the LGBTQ Equality Movement*. London: André Deutsch.

University of Leicester's Centre for Hate Studies (2019) 'The Leicester Hate Crime Project: Findings and conclusions.' Available from: https://le.ac.uk/hate-studies/research/the-leicester-hate-crime-project/our-reports (accessed: 27 August 2019).

YouGov (2019) *Explore what the UK thinks*. Available from: https://yougov.co.uk/topics/overview/ratings (accessed 12th July 2019).

Webb, R. (2017) *How Not To Be a Boy*. Edinburgh: Canongate Books.

Witcomb, G., Bouman, W.P., Brewin, N., Richards, C., Ferdinandez, F. and Arcelus, J. (2015). 'Body image dissatisfaction and eating-related psychopathology in trans individuals: A matched control study'. *European Eating Disorder Review*, 23 (4): 287–93.

GLOSSARY

Please refer to the Introduction where we discuss the limitations of language and how terminology is required, yet can equally be inhibitive with the potential to cause offence. We have included some terms that can be viewed as derogatory, and some that are dated and not politically correct, with an explanation for the purpose of your understanding, so please be aware that these are not all recommended terms to use, neither do all these terms appear in the body of the text, but rather are listed to further the teacher's understanding when asking students to research such matters. You may also notice that many of the terms and definitions listed are not linguistically comprehensive. They refer specifically to the language of relationship and sex discourse with relevance to this book and the context of the topic.

Additionally, while the Glossary could be presented as a series of separate glossaries for the anatomical terms, behavioural terms, emotional terms, and so forth, there is occasional overlap between the terms, so we have taken the decision to keep it as one list except for terms relating to intersex conditions and examples of gender labels, which we list separately in Chapter 2, to further your understanding of DSD and gender diversity.

Abrosexual A person who experiences a fluid and/or changing sexual orientation.

Ace A universal term for any identity on the asexual continuum. Ace is also a shortened term for 'asexual'.

Adolescence The time between the onset of puberty and established biological adulthood.

Adrenarche Early stages of sexual development: normally growth of pubic hair, body odour and skin changes.

Adultery Sexual relations outside of a partnership or marriage that have not been mutually agreed by the people in that partnership or marriage.

Androgyny Sometimes also referred to as non-binary, gender queer or gender neutral. Normally used in describing the physical appearance of somebody who does not present in the stereotypical male/female dichotomy.

Anti-choice A movement in which activists are against the granting of choice to have an abortion.

AFAB An acronym for 'assigned female at birth'.

AIDS An acronym for 'Acquired Immune Deficiency Syndrome', a term used to describe a range of potentially life-limiting infections and diseases when the human immune system has been severely compromised by the HIV virus (see HIV). AIDS cannot be transmitted from one person to another: it is the result of exposure to the HIV virus.

Allosexual A person who experiences sexual attraction to others.

Ally A person who supports the LGBTQI+ community but does not identify as LGBTQI+.

AMAB An acronym for 'assigned male at birth'.

Andropause The decline in testosterone levels experienced by older men that may cause symptoms such as fatigue and loss of libido. Sometimes it is known as 'male menopause'.

Anilingus: The act of stimulating the anus with the mouth, lips and tongue.

Appropriation Adopting something from a different culture for the use of one's own.

Aro/aromantic A universal term for someone who experiences little or no romantic attraction.

Asexual A universal term for someone who experiences little or no sexual attraction.

Autoerotic Sexual excitement generated by the stimulation or fantasy of oneself or one's own body.

Autoerotic asphyxiation Deliberately smothering or strangling oneself to heighten sexual arousal (normally during masturbation) through asphyxiation.

Autosexual A sexual or romantic attraction/intimacy to yourself without desiring sexual activity with others.

Bareback Oral, vaginal or anal sex without the use of a condom.

Bartholin's glands Two pea-sized alveolar glands at the left and right rear side of the vagina opening. They produce lubrication to the vagina.

Barrier methods Contraceptives such as condoms, diaphragm, cervical cap and contraceptive sponge all create a sperm barrier.

BDSM An acronym for 'Bondage, Domination, Sadism, Masochism' or 'Bondage, Domination and Sadomasochism'. Erotic engagement in a range of consensual sexual practices, specifically sadistic or dominant role engagement with masochistic or submissive role play.

Berdache A derogatory term assigned by pre-20th century anthropologists to a person adopting a mixed-gender role in any Native American tribe. Since 1990, the term has been replaced with 'two-spirit'.

Bi A person who has an emotional, romantic and/or sexual attraction to both males and females.

Bicurious A person who is curious about having a sexual or romantic attraction and/or experiences with more than one gender.

Bi erasure (also known as bisexual erasure or bisexual invisibility) An attempt to ignore, remove, re-explain or falsify evidence of bisexuality in academia, history, the news or other primary sources.

Binary The way in which society divides sex and gender into only two specific categories as either male or female, man or woman, with a strict division and dichotomy.

Binding The practice of tightly wrapping the breast tissue with fabric or a specially designed breast binder to smooth the appearance and give the impression of a flat chest.

Biphobia A fear or a dislike of a person or group of people who identify as bisexual.

Bisexual A person who has an emotional romantic and/or sexual attraction to males and females.

Blockers Medication for the purpose of delaying the onset or development of puberty by 'blocking' the testosterone and oestrogen hormones from having unwanted developmental effects.

Blow job Oral stimulation performed on a penis, involving tonguing and sucking (not blowing).

Blue balls Slang term for the experience of sexual arousal and sensation within the testicles when ejaculation is not achieved and the testicles feel uncomfortable.

Body Dysmorphic Disorder (**BDD**) A mental health condition in which a person spends an excessive or debilitating amount of time worrying or feeling distressed by parts of their physical appearance.

Bottom surgery Surgery involving the genitalia, rather than the rectum or anus.

Butch A lesbian who is considered to have masculine traits, behaviours, mannerisms, and so forth.

Calabai/Calalai A person who identifies as 'two-spirit' in Indonesian culture. Note that 'two-spirit' is a contested Western sociological interpretation of non-Western cultures.

Camp An extravagant or theatrical expression, relating to the traits, behaviours, mannerisms, and so forth, considered to be of an effeminate nature.

Cervix Narrow passage forming the lower end of the uterus.

Cesarian-section/C-section An operation for child-birth in which the baby is lifted out by a surgeon through an incision in the abdomen.

Chemical castration A medical process where drugs are used to change the levels of hormones in the body in order to reduce the patient's sexual arousal or interest in sex.

Chemsex The use of drugs by gay or bisexual men to facilitate sex usually using either one or a combination of mephedrone, GHB/GBL or methamphetamine, drugs that enable users to feel relaxed, yet aroused. https://www.davidstuart.org/what-is-chemsex

Chest surgery Slang term used to describe double mastectomy performed for transition purposes as.

Chromosome A collection of genes, typically associated with being female (XX chromosomes) or being male (XY chromosomes).

Circumcision Removal of the foreskin from a penis, normally associated with religious, hygiene or medical practice.

Cis/cisgender A person whose gender identity is the same as the sex and/or gender they were assigned at birth.

Cishet A word to describe a person who is both cisgender and heterosexual.

Civil partnership A legally recognised union (similar to marriage) between two people identifying as same sex.

Clitoris/clit A sensitive, erogenous organ visible above the vagina, at the anterior end of the vulva. This is the only organ in the human body dedicated solely to pleasure. It is not, in fact, pea-sized as most of the clitoris is beneath the skin including two 4-inch roots reaching down from the gland towards the vagina.

Closet The state in which a person does not disclose something or tries to hide something.

Come/cum This can be used as a noun or a verb. As a noun it describes semen. As a verb, to come/cum describes climax or achieving orgasm.

Coming out The act of recognising and accepting one's sense of gender identity or sexuality and disclosing this to others.

Conversion therapy A form of intervention to challenge and change a person's gender identity or sexuality using a variety of techniques.

Cottaging Participating in sexual activity in public toilets, predominantly between gay men.

Cowper's glands Two small glands on either side of the urethra, below the prostate gland, which secrete an alkaline mucus in response to sexual arousal. This is designed to protect sperm as it passes through the urethra during ejaculation. This secretion is more commonly known as pre-ejaculate or pre-cum/come.

Cross-dressing Wearing clothes to imitate a gender other than that which one identifies or usually presents as.

Cross-sex hormone treatment/therapy Hormones prescribed to a person going through transition to correct their hormonal balance according to their gender identity – e.g. a trans male might be prescribed testosterone and then his hormone levels medically monitored until levels of oestrogen and testosterone fall into the desired range for him to experience gender comfort.

Cruising The process of searching public places for sexual partners.

Cunnilingus Oral stimulation performed on the vulva (sometimes known as the vagina, but we use vulva as this includes the entire genital area, whereas vagina technically refers to the muscular canal connecting the uterus to the vulva).

Cybersex Sexual arousal and/or engagement using computer and normally internet technology. This can be anything from exchanging sexual messages and pictures with another person or wearing virtual reality equipment.

Cyber-stalking Persistent electronic communications used to harass or frighten somebody.

Date rape This is a form of acquaintance rape. However, date rape specifically refers to a rape in which there has been a romantic or potentially sexual element in the relationship of the two people involved.

Deadname The birth name of an individual who has subsequently changed name, specifically used by trans individuals who choose to go by a new name rather than their assigned name at birth.

Deep-throating The act of relaxing the back of the throat to allow deeper penetration of the penis during fellatio.

Demisexual A person who has or experiences a partial connection to one or more sexualities.

Dental dam A latex or polyurethane sheet used between the mouth and vulva/vagina/anus during oral sex to help prevent infection.

DFAB An acronym for 'defined female at birth'.

Dildo A sex toy that is often phallic in appearance. Used for masturbation or with sexual partners for vaginal and anal stimulation.

DMAB An acronym for 'defined male at birth'.

Domestic partnership An interpersonal relationship between two individuals who share a home and domestic life and are in a committed relationship but not married or in civil partnership. Domestic partnership gives certain legal rights honouring that partnership.

Domestic abuse Abusive behaviours that might include mental, physical, sexual or financial torment or coercion and control of a person or people sharing a domestic setting or shared home with the perpetrator.

Donor insemination (DI) The process of a baby being conceived through donated sperm.

Double-penetration (DP) Sexual activity in which one person is simultaneously penetrated in two orifices at the same time. This can be oral, anal or vaginal.

Douche This usually refers to a method of rinsing out the vagina or anus with a pump or stream of water for hygiene, but it can also refer to the rinsing of any body cavity.

Drag king Predominantly, a female performer who dresses in a stereotypical masculine style and adopts an exaggerated male role.

Drag queen Predominantly, a male performer who dresses in a flamboyant style and adopts an exaggerated female role.

Differences/Diversity in Sex Development (DSD) A group of rare conditions involving genes, hormones, genitals and reproductive organs. Also known as Diverse Sex Development (DSD) or Variations in Sex Characteristics (VSC). This can result in a range of intersex conditions (see Intersex).

Dyke A slang term for a lesbian woman that is potentially offensive, although it has been reclaimed by some lesbian women.

Dysmorphia Body dysmorphia is when somebody experiences distress due to the perception that there is something seriously wrong with their physical appearance. Dysmorphia is generally associated with the individual having a distorted view of how they look or are perceived by others.

Dysphoria Gender dysphoria (GD) is when somebody experiences distress due to their biological sex as assigned at birth being incompatible with their gender identity.

Ejaculate Eject semen from the penis at sexual climax or orgasm. Also known as 'coming/cumming'.

Emergency contraception The prevention of pregnancy following unprotected vaginal sex. Sometimes known as 'the morning after pill', a drug can be accessed up to three days following unprotected sex. An intrauterine device (IUD) can be inserted by a physician up to five days following unprotected sex.

Enby This term is used to shorten 'non-binary' as 'NB' is an identity term already claimed as meaning 'non-black', referring to race. However, some people identifying as non-binary use both enby and NB, or neither term.

Endorphin A group of hormones released in the brain and central nervous system having a range of functions that affect well-being, how we feel and how we cope with stress and pain.

Erection The state of the penis when it fills with blood and becomes rigid and enlarged.

Erectile Dysfunction (**ED**) The inability to get or keep an erection long enough to achieve penetrative sex with the penis.

Erogenous zones Ero is from the Greek word 'eros' – to love – and 'genous' meaning 'producing'. The word describes areas of the body that have heightened sensitivity to stimulation and/or sexual arousal.

Escort An escort is not directly paid for sexual acts with a client, but is paid for spending time with that client. How they choose to contract for what they offer as part of that time is a business agreement between escort and client and may or may not include relationship or sex.

Exhibitionism In sex education this term refers to sexual arousal in response to a thrill from public exposure of a sexual nature, and/or creating a reaction of shock or surprise. This might be in fantasy, urge or behaviour and can take many forms, some of which are illegal – for example, having sex in a public place or indecent exposure (flashing).

Extramarital affair/sex Sexual relations outside marriage that have not been mutually agreed/permitted by the people in that marriage.

Fa'afafine A person who identifies as 'two-spirit' in Samoan culture. Note that 'two-spirit' is a contested Western sociological interpretation of non-Western cultures.

Fag/faggot Slang term for a gay man that is potentially offensive, but has been reclaimed by some gay men.

Fallopian tube Biological term for the pair of tubes in which eggs travel from the ovaries to the uterus.

Family Planning Clinic (FPC) Sometimes known as a Community Centre or a similarly discrete name. People rarely visit Family Planning Clinics to plan their future families. These clinics, in fact, focus on contraception and sexual health of all types.

Fantasy Psychological desires that are not necessarily ever acted upon or desired outside of the idea, image or mental concept.

Fellatio Oral stimulation of the penis.

Female condom Contraceptive device made of thin latex inserted into the vagina before penetrative penile–vaginal sex.

Female circumcision The practice observed in some cultures of removing part or all of a female's genitalia for non-medical reasons (see FGM).

Female Genital Mutilation/FGM Removal of part or all of a female's genitalia for non-medical reasons. This practice causes mental as well as physical problems for the victims and has been illegal in the UK since 1985. However, there are still many cases recorded in the UK with reports that the act of mutilation was also carried out within the UK.

Female to Female/FTF A person who was assigned male at birth but rejects that their gender was ever male.

Female to Male (FTM of F2M) An outdated trans term and concept for a person who identifies as, or transitions from, female to male.

Feminine Having qualities or appearance that society traditionally and stereotypically associates with women, such as gentleness, delicacy and prettiness.

Feminism A range of political and ideological movements with the aim of bringing about gender equality and rights for women.

Fingering The use of the fingers to provide sexual stimulation. This is normally used to describe using fingers in the anus or vagina.

Fluid Without having a fixed sense of identity. This might describe gender, sexuality or both.

Foreplay Erotic activity and play, involving more than one person, preceding sexual intercourse/outercourse.

Foreskin Roll of skin that covers the end of the penis. This is the part removed in circumcision.

Frottage Non-penetrative sex. The act of rubbing the genitalia against another person's body to achieve sexual arousal. This can be with or without clothing on and is also sometimes known as dry humping or tribbing.

Fuck Have sexual intercourse with somebody. This can be used as a verb, noun or adjective.

G-spot Erogenous zone at anterior wall of the vagina. This is part of the clitoral network (see Clitoris).

Gaff An item of clothing worn in an attempt to tuck or hide the testicles and penis.

Gamete storage The process of harvesting and storing eggs and sperm for future reproduction purposes.

Gas-lighting Deliberate manipulation leading an individual to believe that they do not have a grasp of reality and must be wrong/insane.

Gay Predominantly used to describe a man who has an emotional, romantic and/or sexual attraction towards other men. The term can be used to describe both lesbian and gay sexuality, with some women preferring to define themselves as gay as opposed to lesbian.

Gay icon A public figure who is highly regarded by the LGBTQI+ community – for example, Judy Garland, Freddie Mercury, Madonna, Dusty Springfield, Elton John, George Michael, Kylie Minogue, Taylor Swift.

Gay Liberation Movement Social and political movement in the 1960s–80s encouraging lesbian women and gay men to come out and end societal shaming of their sexuality.

Gender A state of identification that some people use to describe their internal sense of self as male, female, both or neither, as well as one's outward presentation and behaviours (gender expression). Gender norms vary among cultures and over time (see Chapter 2 for some examples of gender labels).

Gender assignment The classification of an infant's gender based on the appearance of their genitals at birth.

Gender Confirmation Surgery The process of medical or surgical intervention to alleviate gender dysphoria, such as breast enlargement or augmentation (mammoplasty) or breast reduction (or mastectomy), vaginoplasty or phalloplasty, or other forms of surgery (such as plastic surgery or facial reconstruction) to help align an individual's gender identity and their physical appearance (previously termed as 'Gender Reassignment Surgery').

Gender confusion The state of questioning one's own gender identity and feeling unsure or confused about this.

Gender dysphoria A sense of distress or unhappiness due to a person's gender not matching their sex characteristics and/or assigned gender at birth.

Gender expression The way in which a person manifests or expresses their gender.

Gender identity The way in which a person internally experiences and/or expresses and/or conveys their sense of gender to others.

Gender Identity Clinic or GID A centre that provides a range of psychological and physiological support for those referred for treatment of gender health issues. Expert recommendations can include counselling, psychological support, speech therapy, endocrinology (hormone therapy), hair removal, and surgical intervention.

Gender marker The recognition on an official document, such as a passport, as either male (M) or female (F).

Gender normative Representing traditional and stereotypical societal ideas of what it means to be female or male.

Gender neutral A person who identifies as having a gender that is neutral – neither exclusively female nor male.

Gender non-conforming A person whose gender expression does not necessarily match the stereotypical binary masculine or feminine and societal ideas of those perceived roles.

Gender Recognition Certificate A document that has been issued to demonstrate that a person has satisfied the required criteria for legal recognition in their acquired gender, made possible through the Gender Recognition Act (2004).

Gender role The behaviours, position and/or roles that some deem typical for men or women.

Gender variant/variance A person who identifies and/or expresses themselves in ways different from the binary gender norms of society (also known as 'gender diverse' or 'gender non-conforming').

Gross indecency An undefined term in law that could be used widely to prosecute people engaged in inappropriate sexual activity.

Guiche The perinium.

GUM clinic Genitourinary medicine clinics where medics specialise in sexual health.

Hate crime An act of discrimination, characteristically through violence or victimisation against an individual or a group based on their perceived or actual identification with a specifically protected social category (such as race, religion, disability, gender or sexuality).

Hermaphrodites A dated term for a person who has an intersex condition.

Heteroflexible A form of sexual orientation which is primarily heterosexual but may be secondarily bisexual.

Heteronormative An attitude or belief whereby heterosexuality is promoted as the normal or superior sexual orientation (see also Normalise).

Heterosexual A male who has an emotional, romantic and/or sexual attraction exclusively towards a female or females, or a female who has an emotional, romantic and/or sexual attraction exclusively for a male or males.

Hir A gender-neutral pronoun used to replace he/she/they.

HIV An acronym for 'Human Immunodeficiency Virus', a virus that damages the cells of the immune system, which in turn can reduce the ability to combat common infections and diseases. There is currently no cure for the HIV virus, although effective drug therapy can help an individual with the virus to live a long and healthy life. The HIV virus can exist in bodily fluids such as semen, vaginal fluid, anal fluid, blood and breast milk, but not in sweat, urine or saliva.

Homophobia A fear or a dislike of a person or group of people who identify as either lesbian or gay.

Homoromantic A person who is romantically attracted to a member of the same gender or sex.

Hormones Chemicals produced in the body that regulate the activity of cells and organs. These affect everything from growth and human development to emotions and mood, as well as playing a vital part in reproduction.

Hormone replacement therapy/HRT Normally used to treat the symptoms of the menopause. Hormones are artificially replaced for medical purposes.

Hormone Therapy/Treatment Endocrine therapy which manipulates the body's hormone balance for medical purposes.

HPV/Human Papilloma Virus There are around 100 types of this virus, with 30 of those types affecting the genitals, rectum and anus. Screenings and vaccinations are available to reduce risks that can lead to cancer and genital warts.

Hymen Thin skin tissue that surrounds the external vagina.

Hysterectomy Surgical removal of the uterus. This may also involve removal of the cervix, ovaries and fallopian tubes, depending on the medical needs of the patient.

Identity The way in which a person expresses their sense of self.

Impotence Consistent problems with sustaining an erection, causing inability to have penetrative sex and/or climax.

Incest Sexual activity between persons that by law are too closely related to legally be allowed to marry.

Indecent exposure The intentional revealing of one's genitals in a public place, causing distress or offence.

Infertile The state of requiring intervention in order to reproduce.

Infibulation (FGM) Removal of the clitoris and labia, and then stitching of the vulva to prevent sexual intercourse.

Internalisation The conscious or unconscious assimilation of a behaviour and/or attitude.

Internalised homophobia/transphobia The negative feelings directed towards oneself based on sexual identity or gender identity.

Intersex A number of different conditions can be described as Intersex or DSD (Diversity of Sexual Development). (See Chapter 2 for specific examples.)

Intimacy/intimate An emotional and/or physical closeness to another person.

IVF An acronym for 'in vitro fertilisation', a technique to help people with fertility, where an egg is removed from the ovaries and fertilised with sperm in a laboratory. The resultant embryo is returned to a womb to grow and develop.

Jizz/jism: semen or cum/come.

Johari window A technique used to help a person understand their relationship with others, consisting of a quadrant with the horizontal labels 'known to self' and 'known to others', along with the vertical labels 'known to others' and 'not known to others'.

Jonny A condom.

Kink This can be sexual or non-sexual and involves fantasy, desire and practice based on the unique tastes of an individual, eliciting pleasure and euphoria.

Kinsey scale Also known as the 'heterosexual–homosexual rating scale', a measure developed by Alfred Kinsey and his colleagues in 1948 and used in research to describe a person's sexual orientation, ranging from 0 for exclusively heterosexual to 6 for exclusively homosexual.

Labia Part of the vulva consisting of the labia majora (outer lips) and labia minora (inner lips).

Lady-boy Also known as Kathoey. Commonly considered to be a person of a third sex or a person who identifies as trans in some form.

Lesbian A woman who has an emotional, romantic and/or sexual attraction to women.

LGBT Lesbian, Gay, Bisexual, Transgender.

LGBTQI+ Lesbian, Gay, Bisexual, Transgender, Queer or Questioning, Intersex. The + refers to those identifying as asexual, the queer community or people who do not identify as heterosexual or cisgender.

Libido Sexual desire.

Limbic system Neurological networks associated with instinct, mood, emotions and drives, including sex drive.

Love-bite A mark left on the skin caused by the sucking and biting of a sexual partner. A red bruise visible on the neck is known as a hicky.

Lubes/lubrication Personal lubricants are used to reduce friction during sexual play.

Male to female (MTF or M2F) An outdated trans term for a person who identifies as or transitions to live full time as a female.

Male to male A person whose sex and/or gender was assigned female at birth but who reject that their gender was ever female.

Marital rape (**or spousal rape**) Sex without consent within a marriage. This is a form of domestic violence and sexual abuse.

Marriage A culturally recognised union of two people who make specific vows of commitment to one another depending on their unique belief systems.

Masexuality An attraction to men and/or masculinity.

Mammoplasty The surgical enlargement or augmentation of the breasts.

Masculine Having qualities or appearance society traditionally and stereotypically associated with men, such as power, strength and rugged looks.

Mastectomy The surgical removal of the breasts or breast reduction.

Masturbation Sexual self-stimulation of one's own genitals.

Medical transition See Gender Confirmation Surgery.

Milking Prostate massage via the rectum or externally through the perineum for sexual pleasure or medical purposes. Ejaculation can be achieved this way.

Minority stress The stress that those from a minority and potentially a stigmatised minority or underrepresented group may experience in relation to a multitude of factors such as discrimination or prejudice, access to support services, and so forth.

Misgendering Inappropriately referring to a person by a pronoun that does not reflect the way they identify.

Monogamy The practice, or state, of either being married to one person or having a sexual relationship with only one partner.

Morning after pill A form of medication used as a birth-control measure following unprotected sexual intercourse or where protected intercourse has failed – e.g. a condom has split or a contraceptive pill has been forgotten).

MSM An acronym for 'Men who have Sex with Men', a term used by HIV/AIDS researchers to identify men who do not identify as gay but who do have sex with men. As such, the term defines sexual behaviour and not sexual identity.

Mx A title such as 'Mr, Mrs, Miss', but one that does not denote gender.

Nádleehi A person who identifies as 'two-spirit' in Navaho/Navajo culture. Note that 'two-spirit' is a contested Western sociological interpretation of non-Western cultures.

Nomasexual A person who is attracted to anyone who is not a man.

Non-binary A person who does not identify as having a binary gender or perhaps a gender at all.

Normalise An attempt to make something accepted as natural within society.

Oestrogen A hormone that is mainly produced by the ovaries. This guides changes at puberty and other key developmental phases.

Ofsted (Office for Standards in Education) In relation to Ofsted, the new Inspection Handbook (2019) discusses RSE in paragraphs 174, 218, 224, 226, 273.

Open relationship An agreement between people in a romantic relationship that they are not bound by monogamy or exclusive romantic or sexual relations with one another only.

Oral sex Using the mouth and tongue to provide sexual stimulation, normally mouth to genitals.

Orgasm Sexual climax.

Orgy A sexual party involving a group of people.

Outing The act of revealing something about another person in a potentially harmful manner, usually against their will.

Packing Wearing a prosthetic penis or padding in the front of underwear to replicate a penis.

Pansexual A person who feels attraction to other human beings irrespective of their sex or gender identity.

Pegging A female using a strap-on phallus for penetrative anal sex with a man.

Petting Sexual or romantic caressing and touching.

Phalloplasty The surgical construction of a penis or reconstruction of the penis.

Pill, The An oral contraceptive form of medication that combines oestrogen and progesterone, altering the menstrual cycle and eliminating ovulation.

Pimp A person who employs prostitutes and takes a cut of their payments.

PMT/PMS Pre-menstrual tension or syndrome is the various symptoms that might occur in the lead-up to having a period.

Polyamory The practice of engaging in multiple sexual relationships simultaneously, with agreement of all those involved.

Polygamy Having more than one spouse at the same time.

Polysexual A person who is attracted to multiple genders.

Porn/pornography The representation of sexual behaviour through any form of media, designed to provide sexual excitement.

Pos/poz A slang term for being infected with HIV; being HIV positive from which 'pos/poz' derives.

Post-op (or post-operative) A trans term for a person who has had Gender Confirmation Surgery.

Pre-cum/come A clear fluid that is emitted during sexual arousal prior to ejaculation (see Cowper's glands).

Premature ejaculation Ejaculation at foreplay or the immediacy of sexual intimacy.

Pre-transition Adopting one's gender identity prior to undergoing hormonal and/or surgical intervention (or 'Gender Confirmation Surgery').

Primary sex characteristics These refer to the genitalia and reproductive organs.

Privilege The opportunities and benefits that are taken for granted by dominant or non-oppressed groups.

Procreative sex Sexual intercourse for the purpose of reproduction.

Prostate gland The prostate releases fluid that nourishes and protects sperm.

Prostitute Someone who is paid to engage in sexual acts.

Puberty A period of time when a person becomes sexually mature.

Pubes/pubic hair Body hair found around the genitals in adolescents and adults.

Queer A universal term (that can be used in a derogatory manner) which is assigned to anyone whose sex and/or gender identity is unique or outside the heteronormative.

Questioning The process of querying and/or exploring one's gender, sexual identity or sexual orientation.

Rape A sexual assault that involves non-consensual sexual penetration of another by physical force, coercion or when a person is incapable of providing consent.

Real-life experience The process of accepting one's true gender identity and/or pursuing changes to explore and experience life as such within society (see Social transition).

Rimming (anilingus) The act of stimulating the anus of a partner with the mouth, specifically the lips or tongue.

Romantic A form of intimate relationship and closeness to another person separate from their immediate family connections that is of a loving nature.

Romantimate/romantimacy A term to describe a relationship that combines romance and intimacy, generally to describe a loving, sexual relationship.

Safer sex The use of methods or devices to reduce the risk of catching or passing of sexually transmitted diseases/infections.

Scissoring A sexual act in which sexual partners intertwine their legs so that they can rub their genitals against one another (see Tribbing/tribadism).

Scrotum/scrote The pouch of skin that contains the testicles/testes.

Sex addiction This refers to compulsive engagement or participation with any form of sexual activity. However, there is wide debate over the legitimacy of this term as to how one sets the benchmark for what is considered to be a 'normal' sex drive.

Sex change An outdated and potentially offensive term for Gender Confirmation Surgery (see Gender Confirmation Surgery).

Sex chromosomes A chromosome that determines a person's physical genitalia and sex characteristics.

Sex toys Any object, especially of specific design, that is used to enhance sexual pleasure or stimulation.

Sex worker A person who is paid for sexual services in money or goods.

Sexism The discrimination of another based on their gender or sex.

Sexology The study of human sexuality.

Sexting The sending and receiving of text messages (usually via a mobile phone) that are sexual in nature.

Sexual abuse Any unwanted sexual activity, whether physical (such as unwanted touching or molestation), verbal (such as threats) or behavioural (such as indecent exposure).

Sexual activity Behaviour of an erotic or sexual nature that may or may not involve penetrative sex.

Sexual dysfunction A problem that may occur at any phase of the sexual response cycle.

Sexual health The good practice of looking after one's sexual health, which may include taking measures to prevent sexually transmitted diseases/infections; contraception and pregnancy; and relationships.

Sexual history The sharing of information with another about past/present partners and/or sexual activity.

Sexual intercourse Sexual contact between individuals. There is a debate about this term as it technically relates to penetrative sex, which might be exclusive of lesbian women who practise non-penetrative sex or sexual outercourse.

Sexual response cycle The process of desire, arousal, orgasm and resolution phases.

Sexual revolution A period of time in the 1960s, coinciding with advances in contraception, where moral attitudes to sex and sexuality were assumed, with greater equality within interpersonal relationships.

Sexual rights The right for a person to control their own body, their sexuality and their reproduction, without violence, coercion or discrimination.

Sexuality The way a person feels or expresses their close romantic and/or intimate relationships with others.

Sexually Transmitted Diseases (STDs) Also known as Sexually Transmitted Infections (STIs), caused through the passing of bacteria or viruses through sexual activity.

Sex/gender assignment The labelling of a child at birth as male or female, boy or girl, based on their anatomy.

Shaft The body, or corpus, of the penis.

Skoliosexual A person who is attracted to people who identify as non-binary.

Smegma A combination of moisture, dead skin cells and skin oils that can collect under the foreskin.

Social transition The process of accepting one's true gender identity and/or pursuing changes to explore and experience life within an adopted gender role within society (see Real-life experience).

Sterilisation An operation to permanently prevent pregnancy.

Straight A person who is heterosexual.

Straightwashing The act of ascribing an LGBTQI+ character from fiction, television or film as heterosexual or straight.

Stranger rape A sexual assault committed by a person unknown to the victim.

Strap-on: A dildo that is worn predominantly with a harness.

Testicles The testicles, or testes, are the male reproductive glands that produce sperm and the androgen, testosterone.

Testosterone The primary sex hormone responsible for the development of the reproductive tissues of the testes and prostrate, along with being responsible for the development of secondary sexual characteristics such as body hair and increased muscle and bone density.

Top surgery Typically referring to surgery involving the removal of breast tissue for trans males.

Tranny A potentially offensive term for an individual who identifies as trans or transvestite.

Trans The preferred term to 'transgender' and applies to anyone whose gender identity does not match their sex and/or gender that was assigned at birth.

Transition A process of accepting one's true gender identity and/or pursuing changes to alleviate their gender dysphoria.

Trans man A person assigned female at birth but is a man, often not using the trans prefix beyond transition if at all.

Transsexual An outdated term to describe a person whose gender is different from their sex/gender assigned at birth and who has or is wanting to undergo medical transition.

Transphobia The fear or dislike of a person or group who identify as being trans.

Transvestite A person who sometimes practises dressing and acting in a role traditionally associated with a gender other than that with which they identify.

Trans woman A person assigned male at birth but is a woman, often not using the trans prefix beyond transition if at all.

Tribbing (or tribadism) A sexual act in which sexual partners intertwine their legs so that they can rub their genitals against one another (see Scissoring).

Tucking The act of physically manipulating the testicles into the body cavity and securing the penis between the legs with either tape or a gaff.

Two-spirit A term used since 1990 for a mixed-gendered role assumed by a person from a specific society or culture. The term is a contested Western sociological interpretation of non-Western cultures.

Unprotected sex Engaging in any form of sexual activity – e.g. vaginally, anally or orally – without a physical barrier such as a dental dam, female or male condom.

Urethra A tube that connects the urinary bladder to the urinary meatus, enabling the passing and excretion of urine.

Vagina Not what you might think! The difficulty with defining this word is that it has come to mean and refer to more than is technically correct. The vagina is the muscular tube that leads from the cervix or the uterus to the genitals. However, many people use the term vagina to also cover the entire genital area including clitoris, labia, urinary opening, etc., which is not actually the vagina but is in fact the vulva.

Vaginoplasty The surgical construction of a vagina or reconstruction of the vagina.

Vibrator A vibrating sex toy that provides external and/or internal sexual stimulation.

Vulva The external sex organs consisting of the labia majora, labia minora, the external part of the clitoris (or the clitoral hood), mons pubis, vestibular glands, urinary meatus, hymen and the vaginal opening.

Wet dream A nocturnal emission or spontaneous orgasm experienced during sleep, predominantly during adolescence.

Womyn A non-standard spelling of 'woman' used by some feminists to avoid the suffix of –men.

WSW An acronym for 'Women who have Sex with Women', the term defines sexual behaviour and not sexual identity.

X-rated A previously used classification for adult viewing, now replaced by the 18 rating meaning 'only suitable for adults'.

Xe A gender-neutral pronoun used to replace he/she/they. Pronounced as 'zee' and can be spelt as 'ze'.

Yoni A Sanskrit word meaning 'sacred space', 'source' or 'womb'.

Ze A gender-neutral pronoun used to replace he/she/they. Pronounced as 'zee' and can be spelt as 'xe'.

Zedsexual A person who experiences sexual or romantic attraction.

INDEX